before the mortgage

AND TH

ES,

edit
Chr

SIMON SPOTLIGHT ENTERTAINMENT
New York • London • Toronto • Sydney

SIMON SPOTLIGHT ENTERTAINMENT

An imprint of Simon & Schuster

1230 Avenue of the Americas, New York, New York 10020

Compilation copyright © 2006 by Christina Amini and Rachel Hutton

All rights reserved, including the right of reproduction in whole or in part in any form.

SIMON SPOTLIGHT ENTERTAINMENT and related logo are trademarks of Simon & Schuster, Inc.

Designed by Steve Kennedy

Manufactured in the United States of America

First Edition 10 9 8 7 6 5 4 3 2 1

Library of Congress Cataloging-in-Publication Data

Before the mortgage : real stories of brazen loves, broken leases, and the perplexing pursuit of adulthood / edited by Christina Amini and Rachel Hutton.

p. cm.

ISBN-13: 978-1-4169-1358-0

ISBN-10: 1-4169-1358-0

1. Young adults—United States—Biography. 2. Adulthood—United States—Psychological aspects. 3. Self-actualization (Psychology). 4. Life cycle, Human—Social aspects. 5. Life change events—Psychological aspects. 6. Youths' writings, American. I. Amini, Christina. II. Hutton, Rachel.

HQ799.7.B44 2006

305.242092'273—dc22

2005033244

Copyright information is continued on page 229.

To our parents,
for everything,
and for letting us live with them
while we put this book together

CONTENTS

⌒

INTRODUCTION

We're post-college and pre-picket fence. We're technically adults, but we don't always feel like it. Everything—work, home, love, life—hasn't exactly fallen into place as we imagined it would. But we're not ready to settle down, settle up, or settle for less. We like to say we're "before the mortgage."

This book began when we quit our first-jobs-out-of-college and left New York City, where we'd spent two years living in apartments with more roommates than bedrooms, trading stories of awkward first dates and job interviews (how different are they, really?). We moved back to our respective hometowns and started a zine called *Before the Mortgage* to explore the rite of passage we were undergoing: the school-to-work transition. We wrote essays, compiled quotes, and created photo collages about such topics as crazy coworkers, so-called relationships, and moving back in with our folks.

When our parents were our age, they were already married. Most people they knew didn't live far from where they grew up, and they expected to have one lifelong career. In contrast, our friends are pairing off later and later, and they hop from coast to coast, career to career. (The two of us have changed addresses five times in the past five years.) What we thought was going to be a short transitional period turned out to be a new life stage.

The zine helped us answer the pressing questions of an unstable time: where to live, what to do, who to love, how to be, and when to leave. How else could we make sense of a world in which Rachel snuck into the mailroom at *Jane* magazine trying to get a job (no dice) and Christina went out with a guy she didn't like only because her apartment didn't have heat (his car had butt warmers)? *Before the Mortgage's* readers and writers found solidarity in vulnerability; by telling candid stories, we could laugh at the missteps and learn from each other.

In putting together this essay collection, we selected a few beloved pieces from the zine and sought contributions from our favorite young writers: people who voiced fresh insights when reflecting on the issues facing nascent adults. Whether writing about unglamorous temp work or finding the It Guy, they spoke to us, they challenged us, and they made us laugh out loud. To use the words of E. M. Forster, our contributors are "sensitive for others as well as for themselves, they are considerate without being fussy, their pluck is not swankiness but the power to endure, and they can take a joke."

So you see, *Before the Mortgage* has little to do with actually obtaining a mortgage, but more to do with exploring your own vision/version/definition of what it means to be an adult. Those of you who are currently packing up, quitting jobs, breaking up, and breaking down, this book is for you. But those of you making mortgage payments or not yet paying rent shouldn't feel excluded. If you're questioning your place in it all, you're before the mortgage at heart.

—Christina Amini and Rachel Hutton

WORK

STILL AN INTERN AFTER

ALL THESE YEARS

PUT YOUR BEST FACE FORWARD

by David Kolek

Marimart Binder-Paulbitzki, Mari to her friends and still only Marimart Binder on voice mail, was the quintessential temp coordinator. She brimmed with positive energy, clearly terrified of having to get a real job. I, myself, was in a similar state. Having recently graduated from college, I was somewhat eagerly looking for a job but simultaneously terrified I wouldn't find one. So, I did what any reasonable liberal arts graduate does in the face of a tech-favoring job market: I started considering law school. In the meantime, I worked three temp agencies just to pay the rent.

Early on I suspected that Marimart was holding out on me. After an enthusiastic meeting in which she all but guaranteed captivating legal work, she relentlessly ignored me. Soon I was calling Mari two or three times a day, leaving detailed messages that reinforced my availability, flexibility, and sincere hope for work. When she did call back (and it was extremely rare, let me tell you), our conversations had none of the spark and vitality of our first meeting.

Then one day it happened:

"I have a job for you in Oakland," she said.

"Okay." This entailed a two-and-a-half to four-hour round trip commute involving two county transit systems, three transfer points, and a car—something I didn't own.

"It's only for three days," she said.

"No problem," I said, though I was desperately seeking something more long-term.

"It's only twelve-fifty an hour."

"That's fine!" I had recently decided that as poor as I was, thirteen dollars an hour was as low as I'd go.

"Terrific, I'll tell them you'll be there tomorrow. It *is* entry-level, but it's law-related, and I think you'll like it. Just show up on time, put your best face forward, and I think doors will start opening up for you!"

Yes, she actually used those exact words.

The next morning I awoke with the sun and drove a borrowed car to my first transfer point. Two hours later I was five minutes early for duty at the East Bay Municipal Utility District (EB-MUD) building. I loitered in the lobby, learning that EB-MUD handled the water and sewage needs for more than a million customers in Contra Costa and Alameda counties. I fantasized about the heroic EB-MUD attorneys who were, even at that moment, working tirelessly to protect the water and sewage rights of these same citizens. How would I help them in their noble endeavors?

About an hour later someone finally came down to greet me. (It's an ironclad rule of temping that they are never ready for you and oftentimes can't remember why they thought they needed a temp in the first place.)

"Sorry, Jean isn't here today," the woman said. "She was the one who was going to show you around."

"No problem," I said, putting my best face forward with a smile that would have made Mari proud.

"Unfortunately, Jean also has the keys to the warehouse where you'll be working. You won't be able to start until tomorrow, but I'll drive you over there today just so you can see it."

I was about to learn just how distantly this work was related to the law.

We drove to a deeply industrial part of Oakland in one of EB-MUD's decrepit cars. On the way she told me not to leave the warehouse alone, not to leave the warehouse after dark, and generally, not to leave the warehouse if I valued my life at all. It was, as she said diplomatically, "a rough neighborhood." In addition, she warned me that the electricity was known to periodically shut off, plunging the hundred-year-old building into total darkness. But not to worry, there were flashlights at the ready. Finally, she noted, with a bit of candid embarrassment, that several of the fire escapes (perhaps all, she wasn't sure) were padlocked shut.

The supervisor led me down a dizzying array of stifling hot corridors. Very little light filtered in through the filthy windows. I wondered how many different cancer-causing agents I was inhaling with every breath.

"Here's your new home," she said.

We stopped in front of a padlocked storage room. Once again I wondered what kind of legal work could be done here. Then she told me what lay behind the locked door, and it all became clear.

EB-MUD was suing a plastics manufacturer over faulty pipes that had failed everywhere EB-MUD had installed them. Okay, I thought, there's the legal part, but what does that have to do with me and this dingy warehouse?

"I know it's ridiculous, but the lawyers want us to inventory exactly how many faulty pipes we have, so the court knows how much to award us if we win. I guess we've been piling the pipes up in here for more than ten years and there's a lot, probably tens of thousands. Oh yeah, and we also need you to record the length of each faulty pipe—don't ask me why!"

We both laughed at how silly the whole thing sounded.

"Too bad we don't have the key today," she said. "Or you could get started now."

On the drive back she sagely told me to return the next day in more casual dress as "the pipes are absolutely filthy." For some reason Mari had neglected to tell me just how dirty "entry-level legal work" could be.

"See you tomorrow morning," the supervisor said.

"See you then," I replied cheerily, though I had absolutely no intention of ever seeing her again in my life.

When I got home I resolved to let Mari down easy. I dialed her number, and for perhaps the only time I ever called, she picked up her own phone. After sharing one last laugh over EB-MUD's disorganization with the keys, I got down to business and told her I wouldn't be able to complete the assignment.

An awkward silence followed.

"What are you saying, David?"

What exactly was I saying? Was I saying I thought I could do better than counting filthy pipes in a fire-trap warehouse three hours from my house for three lousy days? Was I saying that I felt betrayed by Mari? That our relationship was over?

Yes. Yes. And yes.

"Well, I'm really disappointed, David. I don't think we can work together again if this is how you react to your first job assignment."

I couldn't have agreed more.

I WAS AN ENTRY-LEVEL FICTION WRITER

by Thisbe Nissen

My most beloved creative writing professor in college counseled fiction writers to wait awhile before going to graduate school for an MFA: *Get out into the world,* she said. *Gather experience. Live. Give yourself something to write about.* She'd worked as a projectionist in her youth, scribbling stories in the booth while the movies played. The key was to find a way to make enough money to live and have enough time to keep writing.

After graduating from Oberlin[1] and a lousy month of waitressing and chambermaiding at a summer resort on Long Island,[2] I moved to the Bay Area and landed a highly competitive café job[3] at a quintessentially Berkeley[4] establishment, equal parts liberal and fascist. The owner swore by organics, drove a silver BMW, wore his hair in a floppy bob, and seemed to have a hiring bent toward fresh-faced young women with weird names.[5] I was trained in the way of the café au lait— which was a latte, but was not called a latte, God forbid there be any universal way to read a coffee menu—by Tinker, who poured gallons

---

1 See "819 Walnut," *Out of the Girls' Room and into the Night,* University of Iowa Press, 1999.
2 See *Osprey Island,* Knopf, 2004.
3 See "Mailing Incorrectly," *Out of the Girls' Room.*
4 See "What Safety Is," *Out of the Girls' Room.*
5 See Zagarella, Moët, Wing, Silver, Glory, et al; female characters in the works of Thisbe Nissen.

upon gallons of milk down the drain as I perfected the café's signature swirl of foam and espresso that had to top every cup we served. It didn't matter if it was 8 a.m. with cranky, undercaffeinated customers lining up out the door and down the sunny street—if another barista noticed that your swirls weren't swirling just so, she'd stop that cup before it got to the customer and make you make it again. Coffee and a pastry at this place could run you nine bucks. I felt like a totalitarian pawn when I presented an unsuspecting new customer with his bill. But the café was only open for breakfast and lunch, the pay was better than average and included health benefits (unheard of!), and the shifts were four days on, three days off, which seemed ideal in terms of having chunks of writing time.

The problem was that during the two months I lasted at Café Snoot I hardly slept for the latte-making—nay, the *café au lait*–making—anxiety dreams whose logic said I couldn't rest until I'd made the perfect, ever-elusive swirl. The only writing I did was copious self-help journaling in an attempt to keep myself from having a complete nervous breakdown. My skin erupted in fields of acne. Colonies of plantar warts bloomed on my feet. I rediscovered the bulimic purging[6] I thought I'd put behind me in high school.[7] Before I left California for good on the day after Thanksgiving, I mailed applications to nine MFA programs in fiction writing, so desperate to get out of the "real" world and back to school, and so afraid I wouldn't be accepted anywhere or get enough aid to fund myself, that I paid as many application fees as I could afford. I applied to every program I found even remotely appealing, including one at the University of Alaska at Fairbanks, where even if the winters were long and dark, at least I wouldn't have to wake up every day to the insipid California sunshine mocking my inner misery.

---

6 See half the stories in *Out of the Girls' Room*.

7 See almost all of the stories in *Out of the Girls' Room* and half the novel *The Good People of New York*, Knopf, 2001.

I went to stay with my parents in New York,[8] a city from which I'd sworn my distance when I left at age eighteen. When a friend who'd been studying in Thailand invited me to come travel with him when his semester ended, I found a cheap courier fare and spent a month writing self-piteously in my journal on remote Thai beaches,[9] in Buddhist monasteries, in crowded open-air markets where fruit and sweet iced coffee became my only nutrition[10] save the occasional bowl of *tom yom gung*,[11] a soup so spicy you'd burned its every calorie and more by the time you finished eating. I kept my wart-infested toes bound in white surgical tape that turned black as soon as I walked outside, and I often sought out public bathrooms in which I might cry in semiprivacy. I was a nightmare to be around.

I frustrated my poor friend to such a degree that by the time we flew back to the States in mid-January he'd been forced to confront me intervention-style in a dilapidated guesthouse on the Burmese border[12] to suggest that it might be time to get some help for this eating-disorder thing[13] and to try to end the cycle of crying all day and grinding my teeth to a screeching, chalky pulp all night while I dreamed my anxiety dreams. He was right. I cried some more. But without a job I had only the most basic, catastrophic health insurance. I vowed that if I got into grad school and scored a few years of cheap student health care I'd go into therapy. I vowed not to bail on the therapy if my treatment began to impinge upon my skinniness.[14] I vowed to stop just vowing things and actually do them, at some point.

---

8 See *Good People*.
9 See "A Bungalow, Koh Tao," *Out of the Girls' Room*.
10 See numerous anorexia stories, *Out of the Girls' Room*.
11 See "Aaron's Tom Yom Gung," *The Ex-Boyfriend Cookbook*, HarperCollins, 2002.
12 See unfinished story fragment in file somewhere under working title "Matt and Chair in Mae Sot."
13 See *Maud and Drew*, the novel rejected by every publishing house in the English-speaking world, an early, awful version of which is shelved with the master's theses, The University of Iowa Main Library, 3rd floor, East Wing.
14 See "The Girl at Chichén Itzá," *Out of the Girls' Room*.

Back in New York, mid-January, I got my first graduate acceptance: I was in—and with a teaching assistantship!—at Fairbanks. It was a relief, of sorts. When the rejections started arriving at least I knew I had *some* prospect of someplace to be the next year. But there were six months until school would start, and I wasn't sure how I was going to get through a day, let alone half a year. I started working backward: I called the organic farm[15] in Virginia where I'd worked two summers before (somewhat miserably, I might add, and riddled with poison ivy and the fallout of a few bad love affairs,[16] but I adored the farm, the physical place, and the couple who ran it, and the vegetable-growing lifestyle, and I thought if I could avoid men[17] and ivy I might be okay there) and secured a job for the upcoming season. But that season didn't start until April, when they opened the greenhouses, which still left me two and a half months to contend with, and as I'd be making all of three bucks an hour on the farm, there was the imperative of earning a little money for what was looking more and more like my impending move to Alaska. Which is where my frustrated and well-intentioned mother[18] stepped in and called a friend who worked in publishing— because that was logical, wasn't it? I liked writing, I'd like publishing, right?—and secured her aspiring-writer daughter an under-the-table job at an unnamable schlock trade house near the Flatiron.

For the next two months, amid ever-arriving grad school rejections and the continued assault of various anxiety-induced health problems (and the persistent paranoid conviction—despite test results that consistently indicated the contrary—that my immune system could only be so compromised by HIV, of which I'd surely contracted a condom-defying undiagnosable strain from one of the handful of boys

---

15   See Eden Jacobs's sections, *Osprey Island*.

16   See practically everything I've ever written.

17   See *Ex-Boyfriend Cookbook*.

18   See Roz Rosenzweig, *Good People*.

I'd ever had sex with),[19] I rode the Fifth Avenue bus downtown through morning rush hour and the Madison Avenue bus back uptown through the evening crunch to put in my days working a job that was actually "in my field," which, a lot of people seemed compelled to point out, was more than a lot of people could say. And it wound up being oddly and exactly true: I became an entry-level fiction writer.

It seemed that Schlocky Books Inc. had been commissioned (or some publishing house had been commissioned and then farmed out the work, subcontracting to ever-schlockier houses until it landed on my proverbial desk) to produce a gigantic and ostensibly comprehensive review guide to CD-ROMs. Now, this was 1995. To technologically contextualize myself a little: I'd purchased a Mac Classic my sophomore year in college, a monolithic gray block of a thing that now looks like something out of communist Yugoslavia. I wound up using it all through grad school in blissful ignorance of alternative computing options. I didn't have e-mail until 1998. *Late* 1998. (Once, in grad school, my teacher, the writer Frank Conroy, was extolling the impending glory that would be the digitization of the Library of Congress, the ability to access any book in the world at 3 a.m. in the privacy of your own home. In rebuttal—and probably sporting Birkenstocks and an Indian-print muumuu—I made an impassioned case for the glory of the world that would be lost: the joy of waking up the next morning to remember the book you'd desired at 3 a.m. and walking down to the used bookstore for a copy, getting a cup of coffee on the way, stopping to chat with the bookstore owner, to scratch the bookstore cat behind its ears. . . . Frank looked at me hard. "What are you," he said, "a Luddite?")

In 1995 I didn't know what a CD-ROM *was*. (I didn't actually know what a Luddite was either and had to go home and look it up. "Luddite:

---

19 See—or, no, please *don't* see—horrifically self-piteous poems and mortifying "song" lyrics penned in private journals between 1990 and 1994.

noun, one who is opposed to especially technological change," from www.merriam-webster.com. (See, times have changed: here I am typing away on my iMac, perpetually online via cable modem, a regular functioning member of twenty-first-century society, I daresay.) Apparently, though, in 1995 there existed at least a thousand of these CD-ROM things, because that's how many the compendium was supposed to review. The rub was that of those thousand, Schlocky Books Inc. had only managed to secure actual review copies of about two hundred and fifty. Which meant, *clearly,* that for the remaining seven hundred and fifty they would compile all available press materials and any previous reviews and hire a profoundly depressed twenty-two-year-old anorexic vegan Luddite in Doc Martens and cutoff Goodwill housedresses to write *fake* reviews of CD-ROMs she'd never seen. They paid me ten bucks a pop, and thus I began my literary career.

There's a human instinct for self-preservation that somehow enables us to block out things the memory of which might endanger our survival as a species. Like the pain of childbirth, for instance. Similarly, I think I have blocked out much of those months in New York. I have snips of memory; I recall cranking out my hundred-word "reviews" at home in the evenings and on weekends on my mother's Smith Corona word processor. You could see five lines at a time on a little flip-up screen, and the machine made a noxious, un-turn-off-able beep at everything it deemed a misspelling, like "CD" and "ROM." I remember nights in my parents' guest room tending to my addled feet, religiously painting on wart-searing Compound W, then rewrapping my leprous toes in adhesive like a dancer readying herself for a class *en pointe,* but repulsive. I recall paying New York City movie prices *twice* (almost twenty bucks, two CD-ROM reviews) to see *Before Sunrise* in the theater because it was a relief to at least have the pretense of weeping *at something* instead of just weeping at everything. I remember my mother suggesting I get out and get some exercise, go for a run or something, which felt like a suggestion that I was getting fat, and, like, actually doing something about it would constitute a feat requiring more energy than I could fathom; it sent me, weeping, into a fetal tuck of self-loathing under the guest-bed covers.

The year before, when I was still in college, my parents had moved from the house I grew up in to a new apartment. Around the same time I had buzzed off all my hair, which was now in the most awkward of growing-out stages, and I bought plastic baby barrettes with duckies and poodles and fake pink bows to plaster down the cowlicks on my head. At Schlocky Books Inc. there was a stylish and very-put-together-seeming girl who'd been there since she'd graduated from Williams the previous June, and who looked forward to moving up in the publishing world, and I thought: there are perfectly interesting and intelligent people who make *lives* out of jobs like this. I told people about writing the review of the "Lifestyles of the Rich and Famous Cookbook on CD-ROM,"[20] because it seemed like something that people would find funny, even if I felt completely incapable of experiencing that amusement myself. I remember when my acceptance letter from the Iowa Writers' Workshop arrived, and my mother and father both wept at the news with a mixture of pride and relief at the prospect of a tangible foreseeable conclusion to my year of itinerant misery that didn't end in Fairbanks, Alaska, where the brochure said students tended to bond during the long, cold, dark winters, which I thought sounded romantic and which my parents must have heard like a recipe for suicide. I remember curling, fetal, in bed, knowing I was happy about Iowa, happy to have a destination for the future, but no more able in the wake of this great news than I'd been before it to conceive of standing

---

20 Possibly a subconscious inspiration for *The Ex-Boyfriend Cookbook*?

up and making it through my life until bedtime, let alone until school would start in August.

It was probably mid-March when my parents—who had seen me over the years in some pretty deep depths of despair—got truly frightened for my health and begged me to let them pay for a visit to a psychiatrist, specifically a man my mother had actually gone to see years before, when I was a miserable help-refusing teenager who had reduced my mother's life to the role of miserable parent of miserable teenager. I have no recollection whatsoever of going to the doctor's office or of what transpired therein, only that when I came out I'd agreed—against the vehement protests of the part of myself that railed against what I perceived to be the Prozac-ing of the population, numbing everyone into apathetic acceptance of the miserable world we live in—to try a course of Zoloft, "just to see" if maybe it would help me out at all, just to get through this rough time. . . .

That was ten years and copious amounts of psychotherapy ago, and as I pop my daily 250 mg dose of Zoloft I laugh with humored nostalgia at the girl who was afraid a 50 mg tablet was going to alter her personality beyond recognition. What those 50 mg *did* do in 1995 was enable me to calm down enough to get somewhat rational and ask my parents for the money to go to a dermatologist to have my feet burned and frozen and cut free of viral activity, and my acne tamed with a broad-spectrum antibiotic, about which I had to put aside my huge, grave, moral, and ethical concerns in exchange for the physical, emotional, and aesthetic relief they offered. I took my CD-ROM money and bought a plane ticket to Jackson Hole, Wyoming,[21] where I sat in the youth hostel and read *Frankenstein* until the excavated, cratered stumps that had once been my toes had healed enough to put on a ski

---

21 See "3½ x 5," *Out of the Girls' Room*, and Chapter 4, "Thou Wast That Did Preserve Me," *Good People*.

boot, and I spent a few days remembering what it was like to move my body in something other than a fetal curl.

In April I arrived on the farm in Virginia in a car I'd bought with the remainder of my Schlocky Book Inc. money, an '87 two-door, four-speed, manual transmission VW Fox station wagon. I spent most of April and May in the greenhouse, where I managed to steer clear of the poison ivy and immerse myself in the extraordinarily soothing and rhythmic work of thinning and transplanting flat after flat after flat of seedling vegetables.[22] The only other farm worker there that early in the season—before schools got out and the college kids arrived for their summer jobs—was another girl, and we got along well, and both preferred not to talk much as we worked, or listen to music, or anything. We just divided the root systems of tomato and basil and pepper seedlings and replanted them in new flats with more room to grow before they'd be transplanted into the ground. My hair grew until one simple metal barrette could keep it off my face and out of my eyes. My acne subsided, I'm sure in response not only to the antibiotics but with the reduction of my anxiety. My toes healed into pads of scar tissue; the warts did not return. Working in the fields was tough, physical labor, which made eating big farm meals with lots of fresh vegetables too much of a necessity to be too much of an anxiety. By summer I felt human enough to take truckloads of vegetables to farmers markets and stand by our produce-laden tables, chatting with customers about which heirloom-variety tomatoes were my favorite and how to keep slugs off their eggplant, and when the friendly ones asked me where I was from and where I'd gone to school and what was I going to do with my life to put all this farming know-how to use, I'd tell them I wanted to write, and that everything, and anything, is fodder for fiction.

---

22 See unpublished short story "Early Girls and Better Boys," probably somewhere on the hard drive of that old Mac Classic that has been sitting for years now in my garage in a pile of old potting soil bags, garden tools, and beer bottles that never made it to the recycling center.

REGRETTABLE
INTERVIEW QUOTES

- Interviewer: I see you have a lot of community service on your résumé. So why exactly do you want to work at *Vogue*?
  Me: Good question.

- During an interview for a public relations job, I had to take a writing test, which involved writing a hypothetical press release for a Land O'Lakes butter cookbook. I couldn't think of a damn thing to say, so, just to get the ball rolling, I wrote "Land O'Lakes Tells Consumers Where to Stick Their Butter" for a headline, and figured I'd change it later. I forgot. As I was going down in the elevator I remembered and thought, *I'll never work in this town again.* The next day, they called and offered me the job. (I didn't take it.)

- Interviewer (seeing that I worked for a political campaign): "You like the Democrats?"
  Me: "Yes. . . ."
  Interviewer: "You'll grow out of that."

• I was interviewing for what I thought was a job teaching English to executives in Mexico City when my interviewer asked me, "Are you a virgin?" Turns out, it was English classes "plus"—groping to be expected.

• I had a medical school interviewer ask me if I believed in alien abduction when I told him about my support of alternative and complementary medicine. (Obviously, acupuncture seems to go hand in hand with tiny green men.)

• Interviewer: "Umm, you might want to remove your nose ring."

• My interviewer asked, "If there were a word in the dictionary that had your picture by it, what word would it be?" I replied, "Well, my friends call me 'Action Bunny.'" Needless to say, I didn't get the job.

CONFESSIONS OF A PROFESSIONAL FLUNKY

by Barbara Rushkoff

My story . . . where do I start? I used to work at a high-profile weekly magazine in New York that shall remain nameless. Let's call it *Persons*. *Persons* was a fun place to work even though the main lady in charge was a horrible, horrible woman. Let's call her Mean Lady.

Even if you did a million things right, Mean Lady was the kind of boss who would point out the thing you did wrong. She never said thank you. She never said please. One time she got a freebie bag from the upstairs magazine called *Teen Persons*. There was a nail polish in it that she didn't want. She actually asked me if I wanted it, and when I said yes, she *rolled it to me on the floor,* as if it were a mini bowling ball. She did this in front of other people, but I was thankful for the beautiful nail lacquer, so I got down on my knees and picked it up. That was her way of being nice, and I was thankful.

One day Mean Lady yelled at me for taking a phone message from someone named John. You see, his name was spelled "Jon," and even though I got his number right and his complicated last name spelled correctly, she still yelled at me for putting that *h* in there. So I quit.

It wasn't the worst thing Mean Lady ever did, but I'd had it. Her assistant explained to her that I was leaving because I couldn't work the late hours anymore. There was no way she could tell her the truth—that I hated her guts and would rather be unemployed in New York City, eating rice three times a day, working some crappy retail job, than work for her.

That's when the Mean Lady surprised me. She offered me a job working for three big editors: Wiry Hair Boss with the Temper, Boss Who Wasn't Like a Boss, and Boss Who Didn't Do Much but Was Respected. I even got my own office.

I felt like a caged bird set free. I no longer had to ask permission to go to the bathroom. I could shut my door for the hell of it. I was free, I tell you, free.

That's when Wiry Hair Boss with the Temper entered the picture. He was nice enough. That is, when he wasn't screaming at me to "leave him alone" when I asked for his expense report receipts or calling me a "secretary" when he knew I wrote for the magazine. Wiry Hair Boss made me photocopy old articles he wrote just for the hell of it while asking my opinions on what records to review and then ignoring them. He also went through my mail. He lingered around my office a little too much. *What do you need? Can I help you?*

There were rumors that this boss had porn on his computer. A lot of people didn't like him for it, but I tried to stay out of it. I liked my new job. I liked my new office with the door that closed and locked. Let him watch porn on work time. I didn't care.

Then one day I came to work, and my office door was wide open. All the lights were on. There was a messy interoffice envelope on my chair. Wiry Hair Boss with the Temper had written on the envelope that I should deliver it in person to someone named John (notice the *h,* how ironic) in the subbasement ASAP. *Hmmph,* I thought. I am not a messenger. Going to the subbasement was not something I wanted to do.

So I called this John to ask him to come pick up his stupid envelope. Only nobody answered. Boss Who Wasn't Like a Boss came by and told me not to "wander off anywhere" (exact words) because I needed to answer his phone. That meant no trip to the subbasement. Saved!

Unfortunately, John never picked up his phone. When I called to the assistant in charge of the subbasement area, she told me that John was indeed there. I should just come by and put the envelope on his seat. But that's not what Wiry Hair Boss with the Temper wanted. He wanted me to hand-deliver the package to John. He had underlined his instructions on the envelope three times. And as anyone knows, three underlines means business.

I decided to rewrap the package in a nice clean envelope. I wrote "hand-delivered" on it with the time of delivery. Thing is, when I opened the envelope, marijuana joints fell out. *What?* That made me mad. I didn't care that he was smoking pot, but I was pissed that he thought I should hand-deliver it to the subbasement. What nerve!

I called my cool friend who worked at a rock magazine to see if I was overreacting. She assured me that I shouldn't deliver the goods. The problem was that Wiry Hair Boss with the Temper was in a closed meeting on another floor and couldn't be disturbed, so I couldn't go in to him and be all Whitney on his ass. If only! So I did the next best thing. I went in to my supervisor, and she told me that she'd have to tell Mean Lady because this was a "hot issue." I went back to my office and closed the door so I could think.

Two minutes later I was summoned to Mean Lady's office. My supervisor had told her everything. There was someone from Human Resources there as well as the company lawyer. Uh-oh. Everyone, including Mean Lady, was very nice to me. I didn't like it.

"I hope you're not gonna fire Wiry Hair Boss with the Temper," I said.

"Don't you worry," they all said.

They wanted to know if I was okay, like the envelope might have bitten me or something. I assured them that I was fine, that I didn't care who smoked what and where, but that my name wasn't Huggy Bear and it wasn't in my job description to deal drugs. They all smiled at me, and then told me to take the rest of the day off. It was 11:30 a.m. They also told me not to talk to anyone.

That's where I made my mistake. I told one person. *One.* Someone I trusted. Note to self: One person is too many. She told one person and so on and so on and so on, like that old-fashioned hair product commercial. By the time I got to work the next day, all kinds of stories were circulating. Was it heroin? How long had I been doing it? Was he hiding his stash in my office?

No one had it right. No one except for a big New York City newspaper. They called me to verify things. I hung up the phone. They called back. I pleaded with them to leave my name out of it. The reporter read her story to me, and I was all over it. My name, my job, my zine. How'd they get that information? Oh my God, Boss Who Wasn't Like a Boss must've have told them! I had told him about Wiry Hair Boss with the Temper in confidence because I thought he was my pal. My stomach sank. I felt sick. So I made a deal with the reporter. I gave her facts, and she took my name out of it. First thing I did right.

Some people openly gave me the thumbs-up on the firing of Wiry Hair Boss with the Temper, which really didn't make me feel good at all. I never meant for anyone to get sacked. Others called me a rat—not to my face, of course (because the people at *Persons* only said those kinds of things when they were editing stories in the notes section of Word, where everyone could read them)—but they stopped saying hello to me in the hallway. Mean Lady went back to being mean and decided not to give me a Christmas bonus that year.

After a little while Wiry Hair Boss with the Temper told me through Boss Who Wasn't Like a Boss (who I was now calling Pretend-Friend Boss) that it was actually a blessing that he was fired. He hated *Persons* magazine and promptly got a job across the street at another magazine. Pretend-Friend Boss left to become editor of an important magazine, and Boss Who Didn't Do Much but Was Respected also left. There were no hard feelings between them and me. But the other people at work? They are still mad at me to this day, and I don't even work there anymore! I wish I had called a meeting with them in my office to tell them that delivering drugs for your boss, no matter how cool he/she is, is not cool at all. I wanted to say, "What if it was your daughter or your girlfriend who was asked to do this?" But I never did, and I regret that.

I hung around for another year or so until I left the job at *Persons*. After coming home one morning at 4 a.m. with my story still not entirely finished, I decided it was time to leave. I was tired of worrying about things like where commas go and if there should be apostrophes in things, so I summoned the same verve I had when I originally "quit" years before. I quit for good.

Sometimes I miss reading all the background files on the stuff that we never printed for legal reasons. But I don't really miss anyone there. Which makes me think that maybe I'm not a *Persons* people after all.

GETAWAY

as told to Ariana Lamorte

With the assistance of a Palo Alto nanny agency, I underwent a nine-part interview process and an FBI background check before beginning my monthlong trial period as a daytime caregiver for an eight-month-old. I joined three other paid house staff—Personal Assistant, Personal Shopper, and Night Nurse—in assisting a Bay Area family of three.

Meet My Employer:

- This family keeps their food and beverages alphabetically categorized in the refrigerator. I wouldn't have noticed, but the personal assistant mentions that one of my duties is to make sure that there are always enough beverages, which need to be stocked and refilled in a very specific manner. Hansen's sodas are not filed by *H*, but by individual flavor name, such as *M* for mandarin lime.

- They have names for all of their houses; I think these people have about twenty. One is named Dwight. I don't know why—I assume it's some kind of inside sexual joke. They call one of their houses Getaway because all of their friends said, "Oh, what a perfect getaway," when the family thought about buying it.

- For some reason, they've chosen twelve as the magic number of Post-it pads needed in the drawer. One of my tasks is to make sure that they have enough Post-it pads. (I remember looking through the drawers and finding eleven pads. I thought, *If they want twelve at all times, should I order a new set of twelve? Or should I wait until they are down to three?* Then I thought, *I can't believe I'm thinking about this.* I e-mailed the personal assistant on the laptop they provided me to ask her about the Post-its. *What was happening to me?*)

- They only use Swedish diapers. (They are in the process of getting rid of all the non-Swedish diapers by throwing them away.)

- They order an eggplant-colored Lexus for the nanny. Since the family will not pick up the new car, two staff members will have to drive to the Lexus dealership. All three of us are horrified by the thought of being seen driving this car. The personal shopper and personal assistant flip a coin to see who will drive the old car home, and who will drive the new car home.

- Mom asks me to go through the baby's clothes for the next three years and start categorizing them by age. She stands in the room, directing me, "No, no, no. Not that one. The pink one. The crocheted one." I move baby clothes into small stacks according to her command.

- Dad leaves on Saturday mornings with his guitar and doesn't return for twelve hours. Mom leaves in a separate car because she says she has to do some shopping. One day while they were gone— I wasn't trying to snoop or anything—I saw Mom's dream coaching journal on the counter. In response to the question "What is your greatest dream?" she had written, "To win a Nobel Prize, Academy Award, whatever." It was the "whatever" part that really got me.

- Mom asks me, "Would you mind picking up a couple things?" I say, "Sure," because how many things, really, could one family buy?

(Later I learned that UPS drivers have a special code for these people.) Soon I am trying to order film for their Kodak Instant camera (though a lawsuit between Polaroid Corporation and Eastman Kodak Company has made it virtually unavailable) and researching a water filtration system. All tasks are tracked via a Nanny Projects spreadsheet (fig. 1, pages 28–29).

Who were these people? Were there any aspects of their life they hadn't hired out? Why did they spend more time tracking the Swedish diaper rollout than burping their baby? After spending Mother's Day with Baby while Mom went to the mall, I quit. It was just too much. I had to make my getaway.

NANNY PROJECTS SPREADSHEET (Fig. 1)

Priority	Owner	Project Description
A+	J	Find a new weekend nanny.
A	J	Remove all non-Swedish diapers from diaper bags. Order more diapers.
A	J	Find fragrance-free antibacterial wipes to include in diaper bags.
A+	J	Figure out problems with baby monitor.
A	J	Diagram the layout of the furniture for Ella's new room at Getaway.
A	J	Copy contents of Melissa & Jeff's wallets for prevention of identity theft.
A	J	Order more trash compactor bags.
A	J	Purchase belt buckles for Jeff.
A	J	Order another sling from New Native.
B	J	Exchange onesie at Nordstrom. Exchange outfit at babyGap.
B	J	Purchase six more silk hangers for Ella's closet.
B	J, M & S	Look for a dry cleaner who can clean suede without it stinking.
B	J	Help with second draft of emergency plan.
B	J	When appropriate, rewash all of Ella's belongings at Getaway that were exposed during asbestos removal.
B	J	Order two cutting boards from Williams-Sonoma (size 28.5" x 24" x 2").

Status	Comments from Melissa
Moving ahead with trial period with Courtney.	OK.
Ordered more so we won't run out. Due to arrive next week.	Good.
Ordered samples, on backorder. Will arrive in a couple of weeks. Also purchased another kind at Target—on my shelf.	OK. Delete this one. We will try the samples you ordered. Otherwise, just go with the Handi Wipes that are in the diaper bags.
Hopefully, I figured out why the sound has been reduced. Next week I will work on the amplifier/microphone problem.	OK.
Completed on 5/2. Left on shelf.	Thank you!
Made copies of Melissa's wallet contents. Still need to get Jeff's.	Try on Tuesday night when you are here for dinner.
Arrived on 5/7.	OK.
Purchased some, showed to Jeff. He said they should work.	OK.
	It might be too hot for summer. Cancel.
New onesie to arrive from Nordstrom sometime next week. Made exchange at babyGap; new items due to arrive sometime next week.	Received all.
Ordered from Land of Nod on 5/9.	Received.
	Call the company I asked you to.
Penelope has a lead on an alternative.	

OUTSTANDING INTERN MOMENTS

- When I interned at a daily newspaper, I was assigned the 4 p.m. to midnight shift. My sole duty was to sit by the fax machine and wait for people to die so I could write their obituaries. For practice, they made me write my own obituary first.

- On a movie set I had to break off the bottom of a beer bottle so it would look like a bottle from a bar fight. It took me two hours with a pickax. It's harder than you might think.

- One time I agreed to feed my boss's cats for the weekend, and then completely forgot to do so.

- I dated someone I met on the job. When he introduced me to his friends, he made sure to point out that he was "dating the intern."

- I worked with another intern who was simultaneously applying to journalism school, medical school, law school, and for a Fulbright.

- I had to write the name of each product in a six-hundred-item catalog on a separate Post-it note.

- The boss yelled out of his office to me, "Hey, young intern!"

- I was working at a public television station, interviewing a man who reached for my notebook, read my questions, and told me how bad they were. "This is what you're asking me?" he said. "You're never going to be a reporter." He went on to feed me what he thought were better questions.

- The sole employee of a nonprofit arts organization told me that he was really glad I was going to start interning there; otherwise, he'd be "lying on the floor, taking naps every afternoon."

PORTRAIT OF THE BAGEL
AS A YOUNG MAN

by Thomas Beller

His hands were large. My résumé lay flat on his desk. He had cleared a space amid the clutter, and he ran one of those big, sensitive, but also violent-looking hands over it again and again while he studied it, as though his hand were a scanner and would impart some key bit of information that reading never could. I later discovered that this was in fact what he was doing—he couldn't read very well, and seemed to place as much importance in a document's texture as in its contents.

The boss—sitting behind an impossibly cluttered desk, in an impossibly cluttered room, with the sound of the bagel factory in full swing upstairs, churning away with the noise of a ship's engine—looked down at the résumé and chewed thoughtfully on his lower lip. Then he abruptly looked up with the penetrating, profound, and fired-up expression of a prosecutor who is about to ask the question on which the whole case would turn. He said: "If someone buys three dozen bagels, and they get a free bagel for every dozen, how many would you give them?"

I thought I heard everyone else in the room collectively catch their breath. There were five of them crammed into the tiny space. They had given me a cursory once-over when I walked in, but now I could feel their eyes upon me. I had seen the ad in the *New York Times*, and it occurred to me that I was part of a long parade of applicants that had come through the office that day. I wondered whether it had been on this question that they had stumbled, one after another.

"Thirty-nine," I said.

Mr. H didn't respond. He went back to studying my résumé, chewing his lips and running that large hand over it again and again. Then he looked up at me.

"Are you Jewish?" he said.

I like bagels, but I never craved them, never viewed them as something special, out of the ordinary, or exotic. They were a fact of life, personified, when I was growing up, by the local store that baked and sold them, H&H Bagels, on Eightieth Street and Broadway, which was open twenty-four hours a day, seven days a week. Besides selling bagels, the store performed a kind of community service by perfuming the air in its vicinity with the smell of baking bread, which gave the chaotic stretch of Broadway north of Seventy-ninth Street a neighborly, friendly feel. There is something about the smell of baking bread, in its diffuse form, that civilizes people.

Once, during an autumn college break, I was walking along Broadway late at night on the way home from a party when an unexpected snow began to fall. It was exhilarating and beautiful, and I rhapsodized about the beauty of the city and of the snow, paid careful attention to the little clumping sounds of my feet on the whitening sidewalk, and scarcely noticed that I was cold.

Then, after a few blocks, I noticed. I progressed very quickly through the various stages of cold until I felt on the verge of freezing to death. I walked faster. I had no money in my pocket for a cab, just a couple of quarters, and with each block the distance home seemed to increase.

And then, amid dark and shuttered Broadway, there appeared an oasis of light and warmth—H&H Bagels.

A lone cashier stood behind her register, white paper cap atop her head.

"What's hot?" I said.

Behind the cashier was the oven, and just then one of the bakers in his white uniform slid a wooden platter into the maw of the oven and removed a squadron of steaming plain bagels, which he dumped into a wire bin. My two cold coins were enough for a hot bit of sustenance. The bagel burned my numb fingers. I walked the rest of the way home with the warm dough permeating my senses.

It was this kind of memory—vague, nostalgic, innocent—that had sprung to mind that day in early September 1992 when, amid a bleak session of scanning the *New York Times* help-wanted ads, I came across an ad placed by a bakery that identified itself as being located on the Upper West Side.

I looked up and thought, What other bakery is located on the Upper West Side? And then I ran to a fax machine with my résumé.

At that time I was a fledgling writer with a graduate degree, a couple of publications, and a few jobs under my belt—bike messenger, gallery assistant, office temp. I took these jobs to make money, but there was also an aspect of penance to them. I don't know exactly for what sin I was repenting. Maybe the sin of having gone to graduate school for writing. On some level I saw these jobs as a kind of karma insurance. It was a way of testing myself: You want to be a writer? Can you handle this? How about *this*?

I wasn't so noble and pure-minded about literature that it was my only interest. I also played drums in a rock band, and I took these temporary jobs because it seemed that, on any given week, everything could change, we could sign a deal, record, go on tour. I wanted to pay

the bills, take things a week at a time, and be ready for the big break. I
was still high from a two-month road trip/tour the band had taken two
years earlier. When that was over I only wanted to do it again. At the
time it seemed inevitable, but two years later it was fading in the gauzy
haze of fantasy, and I was descending into a panic.

I don't want to romanticize this panic. I think the breaking wave of
the present tense is always accompanied by a whitecap of panic, as
true of the moment of this writing as it was then, when I was looking
for a job to pay the rent and wondering what the hell was going to happen next with everything that was important to me.

I got the job, in spite of being Jewish. Besides being the truth, this
seemed to be the expedient answer when applying for a job at a kosher
bagel factory, but it turned out that it was a minor liability. Mr. H was
worried I might demand to be let off on each and every one of the
many holidays—apparently some long-ago employee had given him all
kinds of headaches on this matter.

My job didn't have a title, but I knew right away that it was special.
I was to be in charge of inventory, which seemed a position of consid-
erable gravity, as it included all sorts of items out of which the bagels
were made (poppy seeds, raisins, sesame seeds, sourdough, salt, sugar),
and I was to be paid ten dollars an hour, which I intuited was at the
very high end of the pay scale at H&H. I was also to function as a kind
of right-hand man to Mr. H, which meant, among other things, that I
had to arrive at eight in the morning and call a series of automated
voice-mail systems belonging to several different banks, get that day's
balance on several different accounts, and write it all out for him so it
was there as soon as he sat down at his desk at nine.

My immediate superior was a young man named Rick, a lapsed
classical trumpet player from Buffalo, whose blond hair was cut

Marine-short and whose glasses had small round rims that made him seem efficient and fastidious. His career had ground to a halt several years earlier when he stood backstage at a recital and found that he was incapable of going onstage. Rick had been at the bagel factory for three years and was in the midst of an extremely gradual exit. He commenced exiting, as far as I could tell, almost as soon as he got there, and it seemed possible the process still had another year or so left in it.

Rick showed me around the ground floor, where the bagel-making took place, and the downstairs, a dungeonlike space illuminated by bare lightbulbs dangling from the ceiling. There was one long hallway, which led to a series of crevices that were used for storage, for locker rooms, for the mechanic's room.

Descending the stairs from the ground floor to the basement felt like entering another world. Each stair had a rounded edge, worn down from years of use. At the bottom of the stairs was a long passageway where one was immediately in full view of Mr. H sitting behind his desk, way at the other end. The first time I went down those stairs, I was brought up short by a very peculiar image: a pipe leading straight down from the ceiling spewing water into a white porcelain sink. The water splashed into the sink, careened around the white porcelain, and disappeared down the drain.

"What the hell is that?" I asked Rick.

"It's water from the oven, to cool the engines. It just pours down twenty-four hours a day, seven days a week. It never stops." This was a metaphor. For something. I hoped not for my time at H&H bagels.

Rick taught me the ropes.

Concerning perks: All the bagels you want, for free.

Concerning theft: You cannot steal money, but you can steal food (tuna fish, lox, orange juice, soda, ice cream). It was tacitly acceptable for us—the exalted, white, downstairs-dwelling, Mr. H's right-hand men—to do it, but the Puerto Ricans who worked upstairs were strictly forbidden, so as a matter of courtesy we should make a point of being surreptitious.

Concerning Mr. H: Sporadically bighearted but for the most part a hard-ass in the mold of a boss who has worked his way up from the bottom. He was a Vietnam vet. A Puerto Rican from the Bronx, the youngest of eight kids, he had converted to Judaism when he got married. Some of his brothers and other relatives peppered the staff, but they got no preferential treatment, no extra pay. His oldest brother arrived at the factory in the small hours to load his truck with bagels for his delivery route. Mr. H himself had started out as a driver for the previous owners of the bakery.

There was a certain artistic quality to the precise movements of the bakers upstairs, the way they pushed slats of "doughs" into the ever-rotating carousel inside the ovens, and then flipped them, and then later removed them, but Rick assured me that Mr. H was the best, fastest, most dexterous baker at H&H and that he had once stayed up for twenty-four hours helping bake a special order, which he then single-handedly drove down to Philadelphia on no sleep.

Days turned into weeks. I could feel myself falling, gleefully falling into H&H Bagels, into its reality, reveling in the sheer *physicality* involved in making such a delightfully tangible thing, the sensuous, arduous, choreographed world of the bagel factory.

And nothing entranced me more than the huge, ancient ledger book in which all the inventory details were recorded, a book that would come to dominate my days, and eventually my nights as well.

When I saw that huge, decrepit, almost biblical-looking ledger book in Rick's hands, filled with tiny numerical entries, my heart leapt with recognition.

The ledger book became my domain. I studied it. In the mornings I wandered around the factory with the thing open in my arms, a pencil behind my ear, counting. All around me was the chaos of the men in white uniforms making bagels—the roar of the oven and, at the other end of the floor, the dough mixer, a hilarious machine into which huge globs of dough were fed and which then spat out measured dough sausages. A conveyor belt to another machine, which grabbed these dough sausages, rolled them into a loop, and dropped the loops onto another conveyor belt. A team of men stood at the end of the conveyor belt and, with expertly Chaplinesque efficiency, plucked them off one at a time and placed them on wood platters.

Other men took the platters to a boiling cauldron and dumped the dough loops in. Still other men fished them out with a wire scoop the size of a shovel. They flung the dough loops down a moist steel gully, a bit like shuffleboard, where another crew took the boiled rings and placed them on wooden slats. Then another group of men took the slats and expertly shoved them into the oven, which had within it a continuously rotating carousel, onto which slats were pushed or flipped, and from which bagels were removed and dumped into large wire bins. The bins were then placed next to an open side door, where a huge industrial fan blew on them to cool them off.

Thus: the bagel smell on Broadway.

I counted the fifty-pound bags of poppy seeds, sesame seeds, caraway seeds, sourdough, pretzel salt, and regular salt. I counted boxes of cinnamon and raisins. I counted the number of whitefish salads, the kippered salmon salads, the tuna fish salads, and the jars of pickled herring. I counted the number of sliced lox packages, nova packages, and the whole whitefish (complete with their head, and the one dead golden eye that stared at me while I counted).

I counted the Tropicana orange juice (Original, Homestyle, Grove) and the grapefruit juice and the sodas. I counted the frozen fruits and Häagen-Dazs in the freezer up front. I counted the number of mop heads, broom handles, Brillo pad boxes, and Ajax. I counted coffee cup lids, coffee cups, and the little plastic sticks people used to stir their coffee (a thousand to a box). I counted plastic forks and spoons and knives. I counted napkins, paper towels, and rolls of toilet paper. I counted the number of white paper bags, the ones that held two bagels and the ones that held four, and six, and a dozen (plus the free extra one). I put on a coat and a scarf and a hat and entered the walk-in freezer, which held a galaxy of cream cheese products so diverse my mind reeled. I searched out the smallest, most minute things and counted them, entered the number in the ledger, and later compared the current number to the one a few days ago to determine our rate of use and to figure out how much more to order. These long periods of contemplating the ledger book were probably the closest I've ever come to Talmudic study.

And then there was the brown sugar. Right in the middle of the bakery, like a huge chimney rising from the floor behind the cashiers, was a huge stack of fifty-pound bags of brown sugar. It sat there like a monument to its own importance.

The recipe for H&H bagels is, Mr. H informed me with a wink, top secret. But I feel, given the size and visibility of this sugar monument, that I am not betraying any trust in saying that each and every one of the bagels made there has a dollop (a pinch? a smidgen? a teaspoon?) of brown sugar in it. Twice a week a truck arrived and workers rebuilt that four-sided column of sugar from its diminished status to a magnificent, proud height. When the sugar stack was low, I felt a pang of fear in my heart; after a delivery, I could stare at it for ten straight minutes and feel all was well with the world.

• • •

Downstairs, in a small crevice off to the side of the main office, was a row of desks. I was given one. To my left was Jay, who had been hired the same day as me. He was a slightly built Hispanic man with a thin and neatly groomed mustache, and for the first few days he arrived at work in a long black leather coat, black pants, pointy black cowboy boots, and a huge black cowboy hat. He played trombone in a Latin band that performed regularly at S.O.B.'s and other dance halls around the city. I respected his outfits. They obviously meant a lot to him. He came all the way down from the Bronx, first on a bus and then by subway, and though he spent his days hunched next to me making calls to various delis and grocery stores around the city asking after unpaid bills, he seemed intent on retaining his image as a star trombonist.

But after the first week he started showing up in sweatpants and sweatshirts. It was not a question of self-esteem, but rather of flour.

Behind us, a few feet away, was a huge flour silo. Twice a week fifty thousand pounds of flour was pumped into it from a truck that drove down from somewhere in Pennsylvania, and several times a day an engine revved up to pump flour upstairs to the dough-mixing machine. The pipes leading upstairs often sprang a leak and a fine mist of flour would fill the air. Sometimes it was so fine we would work through it, and after half an hour all of us would be very lightly frosted, as though we'd all gone a little gray. Sometimes the leaks would be more serious, and we would suddenly be engulfed in a blizzard.

Jay's outfits were getting killed. And so he gave up wearing them and surrendered his identity, during that eight-hour stretch, to being an accounts receivable guy at a bagel factory.

The flour storms did not deter Shirley, who sat to my right. She arrived at work dressed as though this were a brief stopover on her way to a shopping spree at Bergdorf Goodman. She was from one of the

Caribbean Islands, had dark black skin, was very pretty, and conducted herself in a regal, aristocratic manner as though her presence at H&H were one of her good works. In fact she was putting herself through business school, which she attended at night.

Shirley handled shipping, and one of my first delinquent acts was to start picking up Shirley's line and trying to engage whoever was on it in conversation. As it was early September, I encountered a large number of mothers who were shipping bagels off to their sons and daughters who had just started college. These mothers were, on the whole, extremely willing to discuss their children.

"Bucknell?" I would say. "Really? How interesting. And what do you think your daughter might major in?" And then I'd get a whole biography. But the most eager conversationalists were those New York expatriates who for whatever reason had moved away from the big city for more pastoral environs, but who were occasionally seized with longing for the old country, which manifested itself in the need for good bagels. "The bagels out here are terrible!" they would say, speaking (rather freely, because it was an 800 number) from Salt Lake City, Atlanta, or Portland. And it was amazing, even alarming, how willing these people were to take the next step and enter into a mild confessional about how much they missed New York, and all the ways their new home was disappointing them, as though to say it to someone who was actually physically on Broadway that very second would connect them more to the place they were missing.

My responsibilities were far-reaching. I drove out to the Brooklyn Navy Yard, where a huge shipment of plastic bags with the H&H logo on them had just arrived from China, and managed to get into an at once acrimonious but somehow friendly fight on the subject of Senator Al D'Amato with the religious Jew who owned the shipping firm.

A salesman from a seed company paid a visit and Mr. H summoned me to sit by his side while the salesman poured little piles of poppy and sesame seeds out on the desk. "Taste them!" he kept saying, while he talked about prices and volume and shipping schedules, and Mr. H did, nibbling the seeds with the blank, unemotive expression of a connoisseur who didn't need to act the part. I felt a surge of pride to be part of the whole operation, and was amazed at the parts of the world with which I now had contact. It seemed vital and alive in a way an office job never could. But at the same time I was worried. This bagel job wasn't what I wanted to be. But with every moment spent thinking about the pretzel salt, the coffee stirrers, and, always, the brown sugar, it became more and more what I was. In November an anthology came out with a story of mine in it, and Shakespeare & Company put it in their window up the block. I stared at it through the glass, and vaguely wondered if I should bring a copy to the office to let them know who I was. But then, they knew who I was. I was the inventory guy.

Shortly after I had begun working, Mr. H called me into his office and handed me a black canvas money belt. He instructed me to put it on and, seeing it was well fastened around my waist, handed me a wad of cash totaling seven thousand dollars. He instructed me to walk the six blocks down Broadway to his bank and deposit the money.

"Wear a jacket," he said, "so no one sees it."

"I don't have a jacket."

"Take mine."

I took his jacket.

All day and all night money flowed into the registers upstairs, and a good amount of time was spent counting it, storing it, and generally organizing it. The place was awash in cash, but this was the first time I had held any of it in my hand. Large sums of bills are so weird, just paper, but with personality. It was as though the green ink of the dollars had some chemical property that briefly stunned me, and for a moment I just stood there on the black-and-white tiles, staring abstractedly at the cash in my hand.

"Take Jay with you," he said.

"Are you worried I'll get robbed?" I said.

Mr. H gave me one of those penetrating stares through his wire-rimmed glasses. He was always in such a swirl of papers and phone cords that when he stared right at you for more than a second it seemed significant. Now it seemed clear that he had understood the true content of my question: *You don't trust me?*

"It's about insurance," he said. "My insurance says you gotta have two people if you're moving more than five thousand dollars."

Broadway was bright with sun and people. The outdoors always seemed especially great and open after a few hours in the dungeonlike confines of the basement office; walking past that porcelain sink, with its water pouring forever down, was like walking past some mythic animal guarding its gates, promising your return. Traffic careened down the avenue, and Jay and I bopped down the street with the bounce of truant schoolkids. The pouch of the money belt was nestled in that soft private place between the bottom of my stomach and my hip, a safe, comforting place. Mr. H's windbreaker fit pretty well. I wore it open.

These bank deliveries were a frequent occurrence. Sometimes I took Jay, once in a while Rick, and on occasion one of the workers upstairs. The tight bulge of the money belt under my shirt became familiar. I felt a certain honor that Mr. H trusted me with his cash. I wondered if he was tempting me. Maybe he was taunting me. Some free time on a crowded avenue with a wad of cash strapped to your gut is stimulating to the imagination. "Where do we want to go today?" I would say to myself as I hit the street, and toy with the idea all the way to the bank.

• • •

One day, shortly after Thanksgiving, when I had been on the job three months and the novelty was long gone, I arrived at the factory at an unusually early hour. The job's intensity had been increasing. "Don't forget about the holiday rush," Mr. H had said to me on a number of occasions. There had been a gradual increase in the general sense of frenzy; we had all the cash registers running upstairs and still the lines stretched out the door in the morning, and again during the after-work rush hour. Those lines made the place seem like a combination of a hit Broadway show and, with its worn linoleum floors on which people stood waiting for their bread, a Depression-era soup kitchen.

On that chilly November morning my thoughts occupied the increasingly rare space in my mind that was not populated by bagels. During the previous weeks I had been on a few dates with a woman I liked. In addition to all the more familiar anxieties, I was careful to monitor her for her feelings about my current job. She seemed to think my bagel career was amusing and temporary. She thought it was an interlude, a funny story in the making. I kept my panic that this was no interlude to myself. I liked her attitude. And I liked her. And she liked me. And on the morning in question, I had woken up at her place.

I emerged from the subway into the cold air of Broadway in great spirits, triumphantly replaying certain moments from the night before, and looking forward to the calm stretch of time when I had the office to myself. It was early, and I bought a paper, got a cup of coffee, grabbed a bagel, and headed downstairs, where I gleefully sat down at Mr. H's desk and prepared for a pleasant half-hour interlude before everyone showed up. But first I made my bank calls. I had come to look forward to the soft, tidy, mellifluous female voice on the automated account information line. I had come to look forward to starting my days with the sound of her voice. This placid image—the solitude, the breakfast, my paper spread out on Mr. H's desk—was so fixed in my imagination that I burrowed toward it single-mindedly, not pausing for my customary glance around the bakery floor to make sure all was well.

And so I had barely flattened the paper on the desk and taken a sip of coffee when Alberto, the night foreman who was just now coming to the end of his eight-hour shift, entered the room and, with the grave manner of a sergeant reporting bad news to an officer, removed the pointed paper cap he and everyone else upstairs wore. He stared at me with his black eyes, which were always touched with a hint of violence.

"We're out of sugar," Alberto said.

He had worked as the night foreman for ten years and earned only a few cents an hour more than I. Like most of the workers upstairs, he was Puerto Rican. He understood my role at the company, my prerogatives and my perks. There was no sympathy in his eyes. I stared at them anyway.

"We ran out around five o'clock in the morning," he said. "I've had thirty guys sitting on their asses for two and a half hours." He ran a hand slowly over his slicked-back hair, as though this bit of information might have, in the very telling, unsettled it, put his paper cap back on, and went back upstairs.

I had underestimated the holiday rush. The ever-fluctuating but always formidable pillar of brown sugar had been vanquished.

I went into the blankly efficient mode of the deeply freaked out. I called my sugar supplier and begged him to let me have some of the inventory that he had already loaded onto a truck headed for other destinations. Then, having been promised enough to get me through the day, I sank into a numb state of dread. I felt a little like someone who had borrowed his father's car, driven around like a big shot for a while, and then crashed it. I monitored the approach of Mr. H like someone watching a hurricane on a weather monitor.

I could only watch the clouds gather and hope the storm was brief.

The gale was of hurricane force. Mr. H just happened to arrive a bit late that day, so it took place in view of the whole office. Mr. H was a hands-on manager. Every one of the myriad details concerning the production and shipping and selling of his bagels was in his head—he delegated with reluctance. And now his worst fears had come true. He came barreling down that narrow alley that funneled right into the black-and-white-tiled room, his face a scrunched-up ball of red. This collapsed-in-rage face was an expression I recognized from my old basketball coach. By now Mr. H would have passed the empty platter where the sugar stack normally rose, he would have seen the idle workers sitting around, the machines all still. He started screaming at a distance of twenty feet. And as he screamed and yelled at me and waved his arms around—all this with his coat still on, his paper still in his hand, his scarf still wrapped around his neck—I could see in his angry features another, quieter and more complicated exasperation: One day I come in twenty minutes late and everything falls apart! he seemed to be thinking. He had a family, but his business was his baby. It consumed him even as it fed him.

He raged on until I pointed out that it was Tuesday. Tuesday was the day I did a massive inventory of the cream cheeses, and the order had to be in by ten-thirty. I put on my coat, my scarf, my gloves, and retreated into the cold humming silence of the old walk-in freezer, the ledger book open in my arms, and began the process of counting, and penance.

I overcompensated, and placed a mammoth sugar order. The next morning a crew of men carried it in from the truck on their shoulders. They made the stack in its customary place. It rose up like a very narrow log cabin, but there were still more bags. They found a place for them in the stairway. But there were still more bags. By the time they were done, the entire factory looked like a World War I trench. A bunker. The staircase, the hallways downstairs, every available space was lined with fifty-pound bags of brown sugar, as though we were sandbagging a river that threatened to flood. Getting to work downstairs meant that everyone now had to turn their shoulders sideways so as to fit through what little space remained. The complaints were endless, though curiously the only person who did not chastise me was Mr. H himself. His was a tunnel vision, and I suspected that the space his body was now compelled to move through was no larger than the space through which his mind always moved, and so he hardly noticed it. All he registered was that we had enough sugar; and perhaps he wanted to give me a break. I was a quantity to be burned through fast and then replaced; just as a basketball coach will drive his team hard at the start of the season and soften up toward the end, I think Mr. H was instinctively letting up on me in preparation for my departure.

Following the sugar disaster, I redoubled my efforts to get out of the bagel factory. I had been focusing my moneymaking energies in what was meant to be my profession—writing. I would make numerous phone calls from my desk to magazine editors, trying to scrounge up some freelance work. There were two obstacles to success in this endeavor. One was that other than a short story that I had published in *The New Yorker*, I had very little in the way of credentials.

The other problem was the dough mixer. With some regularity the enormous engine would switch on, making a sound similar in texture and volume to a big airplane getting ready to take off. This tended to complicate my phone conversations with editors.

"What's that?" they would say when the engine kicked in.

I'm at the airport? I'm at the heliport? I'm at the hairdresser's?

"I'm at work," I would reply, and usually, thinking that offense is better than defense, I would add, "I'm working at a bagel factory."

"Oh, how wonderful!" was a common reply.

At last I pulled my ace in the hole—I called my editor at *The New Yorker*. The flour silo's engine did not turn on. The call was brief. I told him about the bagel factory. He didn't seem to think it was such a bad thing. He was perilously close to joining the ranks of the "Oh, how wonderfuls!" I asked if the magazine needed someone to lick stamps or sweep the floor. He said they had those bases covered. He suggested that perhaps I could do a piece of nonfiction, something short, and asked if I had any ideas.

I blurted out the name of Esteban Vicente, an old painter with whom I was acquainted, who was having a ninetieth birthday coming up and an exhibit to go along with it. Vicente had once shared a studio with de Kooning and had become famous along with Jackson Pollock and all the other New York School painters, but his star had waned. Now he was obscure. But he had continued to paint, oblivious to his professional fluctuations, or at least not unmoored by them, and was now having something of a revival.

It was agreed that I would write a very short profile—more like a long blurb—to go along with a full-page reproduction of one of his paintings.

Suddenly Esteban Vicente became the focus of my existence, along with Euro Disney, which had placed a mammoth order for our bagels. Every day for a week I drove a truck out to a warehouse in a desolate section of Long Island City. The truck was packed to the brim with boxes of bagels, each about fifteen pounds. I would throw each box into the arms of a scrawny black kid who stood on the loading dock and stacked them on a platter, which then was wrapped in a giant roll of Saran Wrap and finally driven by forklift into a monstrous freezer, from which they would be shipped to France for the consumption of European people looking at Mickey Mouse and Goofy. It was arduous physical labor. The boxes got heavier throughout the afternoon. My back was a mess. The skinny guy caught each one into his chest. We didn't have the energy to talk. I kept thinking: I'm killing myself for Euro Disney!

I went to Vicente's studio on West Forty-second Street to interview him. We sat and talked for a long time—I had called in sick, not entirely a lie because my back could not take another day of throwing boxes—and the longer I talked, the more I began to feel that it was a strange coincidence that I should be coming to know this man at this particular time.

There was something wonderfully impervious about him, and resilient. He had a self-worth that in someone else could become vanity, but vanity is always defining itself against the appreciation of others. The only compass Vicente was watching was his own. Vicente was an education in how much single-mindedness is necessary if you want to survive as an artist.

"Like every human being, I want to be loved, but I want to be loved on my own terms," he said. "No one told me to be a painter—it's my responsibility. Artists have a purpose in life, but you must make the effort. Through effort you have joy."

These rather grand emotions did not, however, mitigate my rather craven ambitions to get my piece in print, to get paid, to see my name published somewhere besides an H&H paycheck, and I faxed the article from the bagel factory in the spirit of someone buying a lottery ticket. I had worked on it all night. After I sent it in I put in a good day's work, buoyed by the thought that my days at H&H were numbered. I returned home that night ready to submerge myself in bed and sleep, but not before, just on cue, as my eyes closed heavily, the phone rang—it was my editor, who in his typical measured tones told me, "We liked the piece." He said he would call me later in the week. I slept deeply.

The next day was Tuesday, cream cheese day, and I went about my duties in the walk-in freezer in a state of elation. Wednesday went by quickly. Thursday, disaster struck. I received a call from my editor saying that there was a problem with the art department. Apparently someone somewhere had raised an objection to reprinting a full page of abstract art. Vicente had been asked for a self-portrait.

The man had been an abstract painter for over forty years, and this after a very considered decision to stop painting and exhibiting figurative work. I didn't think he was a prime candidate for a self-portrait. I amused myself with a mock speech I could deliver to him about how, maybe just a few dots with a mouth beneath it, it would mean so much to . . . me! To everyone! Hey, it's exposure! But if there was ever a nonpragmatist, it was Vicente. He didn't give a damn about exposure, and for this I admired him.

I drove my truck full of bagels out to Long Island City, parked it on a side street, and crawled back to lie among the boxes, warm and fragrant (they were all sesame bagels that day). I fell asleep. By now my job had thoroughly infiltrated my dreams: Every other night I had anxiety dreams about running out of whitefish salad. I had another anxiety dream amid the boxes of bagels. I dreamed that I slept in a bagel submarine that never came up for air. I opened my eyes, and the dream continued. This was my life. The fact that it was this beautiful moment of comfort and peace—all those boxes of bread around me muffling the outside world, warming me, the consoling smell—just made it more complicated. Vicente, I knew then, would never do a self-portrait.

● ● ●

Later that day I returned from the Euro Disney job and called my answering machine. We were in the midst of one of the minor flour leaks, and I say being slowly covered in white powder. I got a message that Esteban Vicente had done a self-portrait. I leapt to my feet. I floated through the flour-saturated air. I ran my hands through huge vats of poppy seeds and watched them pour through my fingers as though they were treasure. I went to an out-of-the-way crevice and threw punches at a sack of sourdough like it was a heavy bag, ducking and weaving, ready for my shot at the championship. I was outrageously happy! The piece was on! Vicente would do the self-portrait!

But gradually this elation gave way to something else. How could Vicente agree to such a thing? My elation turned to a kind of mild, sour grief. Had the voice of commerce lulled his artistic integrity? Had he been bullied into doing something for pragmatic reasons? Did he whip off lots of self-portraits all the time and not tell anyone?

And as I contemplated this, I came to realize that intertwined with all my admiration for the man was a little strand of resentment. This is the weird thing that often accompanies one's appraisal of the virtuous— I had regarded his integrity ever so slightly as a reproach. But now, as I considered that it might have faltered, I missed it. I was rooting for it and lamenting it. As much as I wanted the piece to run, I did not want Esteban Vicente to sell out.

The next day, clutching the phone as the flour silo roared in the background, I was told that Esteban had in fact handed in the self-portrait. The magazine had the self-portrait. It was a . . .

The roar of the flour silo drowned out the words. I waited twenty seconds and asked the person at the other end of the line to repeat herself. "The self-portrait was a splotch of red," she said.

The piece was killed. But my seven hundred words landed on the magazine's new editor-in-chief's desk entirely by accident, and found there a receptive audience. The piece was going to run, after all, and she wanted to meet me.

I lasted at H&H though the New Year. Other than a small pretzel-salt crisis there were no major mishaps. In late January I gave Mr. H my notice. He responded coolly to this, but did not seem too upset.

Later that afternoon he had a heart attack. I helped carry him up the stairs, still sitting in his chair, past the porcelain sink into which the endless waterfall poured. The place was in an uproar as we watched the paramedics put an oxygen mask on his face. Among the white-suited workers upstairs, the men Mr. H ruled with a strong hand (primarily by paying them little more than minimum wage, not giving them any vacation time until they worked there nine months, and not allowing so much as the scent of a union to enter the floor), there was a surge of genuine grief. Everyone spilled out of the side entrance to watch silently as the paramedics loaded him into the ambulance. They all took off their hats.

Downstairs, we had to deal with the fact that, at the time he had the heart attack, Mr. H was counting out a huge sum of cash, which lay untended on his desk. About five different people volunteered to be responsible for it. I prevailed. In my dreamy fantasies about theft and revenge I could not have conjured a more enticing scenario. But I counted the money out scrupulously, totaled it, and put it back in a white paper bag (the size for a dozen bagels) as was the custom, and dropped it in the ancient black safe in the corner.

I watched my replacement be interviewed. He had graduated from Deerfield, then Dartmouth. He was an aspiring actor. I showed him around the place, presented him with the ledger book, and informed him that when Mr. H asked him to read something, it didn't mean his expert opinion was being asked, you were just supposed to paraphrase. The rest was up to him to figure out.

Shortly before my last day, I found myself standing in the walk-in freezer wearing a suit. I had an appointment with *The New Yorker's* editor-in-chief that morning, and I was racing through the cream cheese inventory so as to be on time. I stood in the walk-in freezer and slowly counted, enjoying the ritual, the strange environment, the privacy. As always the heavy door to the freezer was slightly ajar. And then, for the first time since I had been working there, someone bumped the door, and the ancient metal bolt clicked shut. I carefully put the ledger book on some boxes of olive and pimiento cream cheese and commenced to bang hysterically on the inside of that door, screaming at the top of my lungs to be let out. I was screaming in fear—that I would miss my appointment, that my big chance would be squandered because I was locked in the cream cheese freezer—but I was also laughing. The bagel factory was clutching me for one last moment in its absurd embrace. And when the door was pulled open at last and I was free to rise up out of that place forever, I felt a tiny pang of sorrow to have been released so soon.

OVERHEARD IN THE CUBICLE

- "Is there extra toilet paper in the closet? You don't know? Because I thought that there was, and when I looked there wasn't. I'll pick some up. It's on sale. I'll get enough . . . not a ton, but a good amount."

- Coworker #1: "Just go to Paxil.com."
  Coworker #2: "What about Zoloft?"
  Coworker #1: "That's not as good."

- "Last time I had a colonoscopy . . . and it felt surprisingly good. . . ."

- "They accused you, point-blank, of being my mistress."

- "Now that I stopped dating the 3M guy, my source of Post-it notes has seriously dwindled."

- "I think Iraq is always a bit dodgy." (My boss at the U.N. discussing future job opportunities with a friend on the phone)

- "Heck, I'll tape my boobs together if that'll help."

- "Yeah, she's great, and smart, and I like her. But she's got such a flat chest."

- "What should I get my girlfriend for Christmas? I think she wants a face-lift, but what if we break up in a month? I don't want to get her a face-lift for somebody else."

- "I just took my pill and will be home in forty-five minutes if the traffic isn't too bad." (Said by a sixtysomething engineer, referring to Viagra)

BRIAN-SENSEI

by Brian Grivna

The five years I spent in software engineering were great, with one exception: talking to nonprogrammers about my day was nearly impossible. Since most of my friends and loved ones weren't of the binary persuasion, this made me feel pretty, well, boring. In addition, the big three-oh was beating down my door. So I decided to do something totally different: I applied to the Japan Exchange and Teaching (JET) Programme.

After one application and interview (during which my fly was down the entire time), I was accepted. I moved to Sapporo, Japan, where I attempted to teach the English language to junior high students who were much more interested in the color of my pubic hair (I am not making this up) than in learning the comparative forms of adjectives.

August 27
Junior High: The Reunion Tour

Junior high sucked. I hardly knew anyone; I was intensely uncool; girls didn't like me; at lunch I sat across from a guy who licked all of his French fries to deter would-be swindlers; and I got my worst grade ever—a D-plus in ninth-grade physics. I also distinctly recall the less-than-attentive behavior of students (myself included) during class. I started to second-guess my decision to willingly return to junior high school to try to *teach* students. But I'd already signed a contract in wasabi-addled blood, so what choice did I have?

My new school: Nakajima Junior High. Several weeks prior to my first day, I met some Japanese teachers of English at a Sapporo Board of Education party. None taught at Nakajima, but they all knew about it. The most memorable remark: "Have you ever watched *Boston Public* on Fox? Nakajima is kind of like that." I was borderline schlitzed at the time, which was probably the only reason I didn't head straight to the hi-tech Tokyo airport. After mulling over that remark for a week or so, I wasn't so worried. *This is Japan,* I thought. *I'm not going to get shot. At worst, I'll have an inappropriate relationship with a female student.*

September 5

My First Day

I managed to drag myself out of bed at 6:30 a.m. Yes, I know, that's not terribly early, but this is coming from a computer geek who was almost entirely nocturnal for a year, so bear with me. I arrived at school around eight, met the staff, gave a very lame self-introduction in Japanese, and chatted with Nakajima's lone English teacher, Mr. Toshiyuki Abe.

Abe-sensei and I taught four classes that day. Each began with my same, very lame, self-introduction, of which the highlight was discussion of the different driving (16, 18), smoking (18, 20), and drinking (21, 20) ages in America and Japan. (I didn't think age of consent would be an appropriate topic—not that talking about smoking and drinking was exactly appropriate, either.) I concluded the self-intro with a Q&A. The first two classes had exactly zero questions.

However, by the third and fourth classes, word of the nutty *gaijin* (foreigner) had apparently spread. I'm sure there was a dossier on me floating around somewhere. The kids all knew my name, where I was from, my hobbies, my home address. They were also more enthusiastic about the Q&A session. Particularly the four girls sitting in the back of my *sannensei* (third-year, equivalent to ninth grade) classes. They played *janken* (rock-paper-scissors) and the loser had to ask me a question.

"Are you married?" one girl asked.

"Do you have a girlfriend?"

"Do you like Japanese girls?"

"Do you like *me*?"

Whoa. Weird. Not wanting to hurt anyone's feelings, I waffled heavily on the last two questions. Weirder still, one of those girls gave me this sandwich-thing at lunch and said, "I made this for you." It had what looked like whipped cream in it. I didn't eat it.

October 18

My Primary Role Is—That's Right—to Speak English!

Abe-sensei and I do lots of corny dialogues to illustrate the use of the day's new expression(s). For instance . . .

Act I, Scene 1: Brian Eats Dinner at Mr. Abe's House

[Demonstrating the use of "Would you like . . . ?"]

Brian sits at a table, pretending to eat.

Abe: Would you like some more chicken, Brian?

Brian: Yes, please! It's delicious!

Abe: Would you like something to drink?

Brian: May I have some milk?

Abe: Of course! Would you like some more cake?

Brian: No thanks. I've had plenty!

In addition to my theatrical roles, I read the textbook aloud, I read things on the board aloud, I read any English I see aloud. At this point it's compulsive.

October 19

Send Polyester!

Kindly recall that I spent the five years between college and JET programming computers, a job in which the dress code is "reasonably clean loincloth required." The business-casual universe is a complete mystery to me, so I didn't know better than to purchase linen pants. You could stretch this crap as tightly as Cher's face and it'd still be a mess of wrinkles. I'm guessing it's troublesome for a veteran ironer, but for a poorly equipped bachelor like me, it's all but impossible.

Anyway, we were teaching the kids how to use "I know . . ." and "I think . . ." and we gave them a worksheet that said:

I know that Brian _____.
and
I think that Brian _____.

Most of the responses were fairly predictable:

I know that Brian is <u>from America</u>.
I think that Brian <u>likes beer</u>.
I think that Brian <u>is a robot</u>.

(All actual responses, all reasonably accurate.) However, one of my favorite kids trumped them all with:

I think that Brian <u>doesn't iron</u>.

November 3

How Do You Say "Detention" in Japanese?

I'm finding that the stereotype of Japanese schoolchildren as perfect, little, obedient, disciplined, respectful, quiet angels with infinitely expandable sponge-brains is, as stereotypes can be, inaccurate. At any given time I'd say one-fifth of the kids in my classes are talking or sleeping.

Last Monday, one student got up in the middle of class, walked to the broom closet, grabbed a broom, left the room, and proceeded to walk up and down the hallway, periodically whacking the wall. On Wednesday the same kid was halfway out the window of the third-floor classroom before Abe-sensei said anything. In almost any American school, I think this kid would be promptly sent to the principal. Not so in Japan. I'm not entirely sure why, but one friend said it's because that would be denying the kid access to education. That is, the kid apparently has a divine right to be in the classroom, even if education is the farthest thing from his mind. As with any culture, some things just don't make much sense to an outsider.

On the upside, most of the kids are great. Most will say hello and/or giggle and yell my name when I walk by. Many want me to eat lunch with them. They ask me questions about things I like. Or they try to speak to me in Japanese, and I feel like a dumbass when I don't understand. They ask me to play Ping-Pong with them, then kick my ass. One student even taught me how to make these wicked origami *shuriken* (throwing stars—you know, ninja shit).

So yeah. School is pretty good. Hardly *Sapporo Public*.

WHERE THE

COCKROACHES ARE

THE FIRST THANKSGIVING

by Sarah Vowell

When I invited my mom and dad to come to New York City to have Thanksgiving at my house, I never expected them to say yes. Not only had they never been to New York, they had never been east of the Mississippi. Nor had they ever visited me. I've always had these fantasies about being in a normal family in which the parents come to town and their adult daughter spends their entire visit daydreaming of suicide. I'm here to tell you that dreams really do come true.

I was terrified we wouldn't have enough to talk about. In the interest of harmony, there's a tacit agreement in my family; the following subjects are best avoided in any conversation longer than a minute and a half: national politics, state and local politics, any music by any person who never headlined at the Grand Ole Opry, my personal life, and their so-called god. Five whole days. When I visit them back home in Montana, conversation isn't a problem because we go to the movies every afternoon. That way, we can be together but without the burden of actually talking to each other. Tommy Lee Jones, bless his heart, does the talking for us.

But my sister, Amy, is coming and bringing her lively seven-month-old son, Owen, along, so the cinema's not an option. Which means five days together—just us—no movies. We are heading into uncharted and possibly hostile waters, pioneers in a New World. It is Thanksgiving. The pilgrims had the *Mayflower*. I buy a gravy boat.

It's lucky that Amy's coming with Mom and Dad. Amy still lives six blocks away from them in Bozeman. She would act as interpreter and go-between among my parents and me. Like Squanto.

Amy's husband, Jay, has decided to stay home in Montana to go deer hunting with his brother. Everyone else arrives at my apartment in Chelsea. Amy and Owen are bunking with me, so I walk my parents around the corner to check them into their hotel on Twenty-third.

"Here we are," says Mom, stopping under the awning of the Chelsea Hotel. There she stands, a woman whose favorite book is called, simply, Matthew, right on the spot where the cops hauled Sid Vicious out in handcuffs after his girlfriend was found stabbed to death on their hotel room floor.

"No, Mother," I say, taking her arm and directing her down the block to the Chelsea Savoy, a hotel where they go to the trouble to clean the rooms each day.

It is around this time, oh, twenty minutes into their trip, that my dad starts making wisecracks like "Boy, kid, bet you can't wait until we're out of here." My father, a man who moved us sixteen hundred miles away from our Oklahoma relatives so he wouldn't have to see them anymore, makes a joke on average every two hours he is here about how much I'm anticipating the second they'll say good-bye. I find this charming but so disturbingly true I don't know what to say.

By halfway through the first day, I discover I needn't have worried what we would talk about, with the baby preventing us from seeing movies. When you have a baby around, the baby is the movie. We occupy an entire entertaining hour just on drool, nonnarrative drool. At this stage, baby Owen is laughing, sitting up, and able to roll over. He is the cutest, the funniest, sweetest, smartest, best-behaved baby in the world.

Then there's the sightseeing. First stop, Ellis Island. The thing about going to Ellis Island is that it's a lot like going to Ellis Island. Perhaps to help you better understand the immigrant experience, they make you stand in line for the crammed ferry for an hour and a half in the windy cold. By the time we step onto the island, we are huddled masses yearning to breathe free.

Our great-grandmother Ellen passed through here on her way from Sweden. We watch a video on the health inspections given to immigrants, walk past oodles of photos of men in hats and women in shawls. Though no one says anything, I know my father and mother and sister are thinking what I'm thinking. They're thinking about when we moved away from Oklahoma to Montana, how unknown that was, how strange and lonesome. I read a letter in a display case that says, "And I never saw my mother again," and I think of my grandfather, how we just drove off, leaving him behind, waving to us in the rearview mirror. And here we are in New York, because here I am in New York, because ever since Ellen's father brought her here, every generation moves away from the one before.

It is curious that we Americans have a holiday—Thanksgiving—that's all about people who left their homes for a life of their own choosing, a life that was different from their parents' lives. And how do we celebrate it? By hanging out with our parents! It's as if on the Fourth of July we honored our independence from the British by barbecuing crumpets.

Just as Amy and I grew up and left our parents, someday Owen will necessarily grow up and ditch my sister. And, appropriately enough, it is on this weekend that Owen spends the very first night of his life away from his mother. My parents baby-sit while Amy and I go to a rock show. Owen lives through it, as does she, though she talks about him all night, which I guess is how it goes.

Thanksgiving morning, my parents take Owen to see the Macy's parade while Amy and I start making dinner. Let me repeat that—my mother leaves while I cook. Specifically, cornbread dressing, a dish my mother has made every Thanksgiving since before I was born. To her credit, she has not inquired about my process since she phoned to ask me if she should bring cornmeal in her suitcase. As an Okie, my mom only uses white cornmeal processed by the Shawnee Company in Muskogee. She does not even consider my cornbread to be cornbread at all because I make it with yellow cornmeal and, heresy, sugar. "You don't make cornbread," she told me, in the same deflated voice she uses to describe my hair. "You make johnny cake."

I'm standing at the cutting board chopping sage and it hits me what it means that she is letting me be in charge of the dressing: I am going to die. Being in charge of the dressing means you are a grown-up for real, and being a grown-up for real means you're getting old and getting old means you are definitely, finally, totally going to die. My mother is a grandmother and my sister is a mother and I have decided the dressing will be yellow this year, therefore, we'll all be dead someday.

"Is that enough celery?" Amy asks, pointing to a green mound on the counter. Is there ever enough celery? Do my parents have more celery in their past than they do in their future? Do I?

I have invited my friends John and David to join us for dinner, and I was a little nervous about how everyone would get along. To my delight, the meal is smooth and congenial. My friends and I talk about the West Nile virus killing birds on Long Island. My father counters with a lovely anecdote about an open copper pit in Butte that filled up with contaminated rainwater and killed 250 geese in one day. There is nothing like eating one dead bird and talking about a bunch of other dead birds to really bring people together.

The next morning, right about the time Owen starts to cry while—simultaneously—my mother jams the bathroom door and my father's on his hands and knees prying it open with a penknife, a cloud passes over me. Once or twice a day, I am enveloped inside what I like to call the Impenetrable Shield of Melancholy. This shield, it is impenetrable. Hence the name. I cannot speak. And while I can feel myself freeze up, I can't do anything about it. As my family fusses, I spend an inordinate amount of time pretending to dry my hair, the bedroom door closed, the hair dryer on full blast, pointed at nothing.

Everybody in the family goes through these little spells. I just happen to be the spooky one at this particular moment. When people ask me if I'm the black sheep of the family I always say that, no, we're all black sheep. Every few hours they're here, I look over at my dad, nervously crunching his fingers together. If he were at home for Thanksgiving, he'd be ignoring us and spending all his time in his shop. I watch him move his fingers in the air and realize he's turning some hunk of metal on an imaginary lathe.

The thing that unites us is that all four of us are homebody claustrophobes who prefer to be alone and are suspicious of other people. So the trait that binds us together as a family—preferring to keep to ourselves—makes it difficult to *be* together as a family. Paradoxically, it's at these times that I feel closest to them, that I understand them best, that I love them most. It's just surprising we ever breed.

The next day, we do the most typical thing we could possibly do as a family. We split up. I stay home cleaning, Mom goes to Macy's, Amy and Owen visit the Museum of Modern Art, and Dad tours Teddy Roosevelt's birthplace. By the time we all reconvene on Saturday evening, my ragged mother becomes so ambitious with her sightseeing that I can tell she's decided that she's never coming back. "Do you guys want to see Rockefeller Center?" I ask, and she says, "Yeah, because who knows when I'll be back again." Ditto the Empire State Building, "because who knows when I'll be back again."

If you are visiting the Empire State Building, may I offer some advice? If you are waiting in the very long line for the very last elevator and an attendant says that anyone who wants to walk up the last six flights may do so now, right away, and you are with your aging parents and a sister who is carrying a child the size of a fax machine, stay in the line for the elevator. But if you must take the stairs, go first, and do not look back; otherwise your parents will look like one of those Renaissance frescoes of Adam and Eve being expelled from the Garden of Eden, all hunched over and afraid.

So we make it to the observation deck, Brooklyn to the south of us, New Jersey to the west, places that people fled to from far away, places that people now run away from, to make another life. It's dark and cold and windy, and we're sweaty from climbing the stairs. It's really pretty though. And there we stand, side by side, sharing a thought like the family we are. My sister wishes she were home. My mom and dad wish they were home. I wish they were home too.

APARTMENT SEARCH HORROR STORIES

- I was just out of school and went with my college friend/soon-to-be-roommate to look at a place in SoHo that was just out of our price range. The *Village Voice* listing said "SIK." That, it turns out, means "shower in kitchen."

- After we'd put down our deposit and signed a lease, the broker gave away the apartment to someone else. When we demanded our money back, he called the cops on us.

- I had a real estate broker drop me after looking at my résumé, noting that I had worked in the lab of Richard Smalley in college (Nobel laureate in physics, discovery of carbon-60). She asked if I could get a letter of recommendation from him. I said no, that asking him would be shameful.

- My landlord was the "dancing bear" at Grateful Dead shows.

- Building manager: "People usually move here after something didn't really work out."

- I moved on Valentine's Day (we celebrated with chocolate doughnuts and boxes). One phrase: man with a van. Man with a van I'd hired had a family "emergency." Instead, man with a van's girlfriend showed up. The woman was petite and helped move a toaster oven. Post–load-up, man with a van's van wouldn't start (maybe because "man" wasn't there). Random Austrian man stopped and offered to help. Austrian tweaked something under the hood and van started.

- My roommate and I lied and said we were lesbian partners because the two-bedroom apartment we wanted wouldn't rent to singles (the current occupants were a lesbian couple who had broken up two years before, but still lived together because of the cheap rent).

PARADISE CONSIDERED

by Evan Ratliff

Looking back, my whole predicament with regard to the perfect apartment grew out of a seemingly innocuous addiction to Craigslist. Craigslist, for those hermetic few who remain unfamiliar with it, is a Web site offering free local classifieds in metropolitan areas around the world. In cities with a strong Craigslist community, you can find nearly any good or service for sale or barter on the site, including, but not limited to: casual sex, employment, workout partners, music lessons, furniture, massages, leftover food, kittens, Bloc Party tickets, and computer equipment. For instance, I once exchanged some Dungeons & Dragons books (obtained from a friend who worked, fantastically, for the PR agency representing Dungeons & Dragons) on Craigslist for a set of video games, which (having no video game console) I then bartered for opera tickets, which (not liking opera) I eventually bartered for a nonfunctional typewriter, which I threw out on the street. Another time, I sold ten sandbags to a guy who announced on Craigslist his intention to live in a simulated World War I trench. He dug the trench in his friend's backyard and spent the night there, wearing a vintage World War I uniform and eating tinned food, surrounded by my sandbags. I accepted a John Denver vinyl record as payment.

The Craigslist feature of greatest importance to any urban dweller, however, is the "Apartments for Rent" section. If you desire to live in a city such as San Francisco—as I did at the time of my Craigslist addiction—and you do not have boxes of gold bullion or Google stock options stashed in the trunk of your car, Craigslist is the most reliable means of finding a home. More to the point, I wasn't actually addicted to Craigslist so much as I was addicted to apartment searching on Craigslist. Every day, and often twice or three times, or many more, I scoured "Apartments for Rent." Sometimes, after thoroughly examining the listings, scanning every apartment in my favorite neighborhoods, mapping the addresses and printing out the information, I would return five minutes later to see what new listings had been posted in my absence. Then I would hit my browser's refresh button, on the off chance that more had been added while I had been busy looking at recently posted listings. In this way, I maintained an encyclopedic knowledge of available apartments in San Francisco. (And also, to varying extents, in New York, London, Amsterdam, and Atlanta.)

Given my obsessive-compulsive level of apartment hunting, you might assume that I did not have an apartment at the time, that perhaps I had just moved to town. In fact, I had a fine apartment, a one-bedroom in my favorite San Francisco neighborhood, the Lower Haight, for which I paid $1,350 each month. Depending on whether you live in Cleveland or Manhattan, that might sound like a ridiculous sum or a tremendous bargain. It was, frankly, a rent more appropriate for an average family of four than for a single twentysomething. But it was nonetheless on par for my neighborhood, a marginally gentrified spot nestled in a happy nexus of nightlife, cheap restaurants, record stores, and public transportation. In that way, $1,350 was the price I paid to easily access all the things that had brought me to San Francisco in the first place. And at the time it was, in San Francisco fashion, barely within the outer orbit of my means—requiring measured budgeting to make rent and stay in the black. I justified the situation by the additional fact that the place doubled as my home office, even though I spent a fair amount of my home office time searching for future home offices on Craigslist.

Overall, though, the apartment was decent, nice even. Both the living room and bedroom had bay windows facing a tree-lined street, and the rooms were connected by a set of glass double doors that might have created an airy atmosphere, except for a hideous two-inch Berber carpet that sealed them shut. The apartment also had a claw-foot tub—highly coveted among apartment seekers but a source of nothing but repeated shin injuries for me—and a pleasantly sized closet. Its only major flaws, beyond the price, were its small kitchen and lack of laundry facilities in either the apartment or the building at large.

My Craigslist explorations, then, were not about finding an apartment but about finding the *perfect* apartment. Or, rather, finding the *perfect apartment deal*. The perfect apartment, after all, is easy to identify: It's a 2,500-square-foot loft next to the park with bay views, a deck, a yard, parking, a dishwasher, a dumbwaiter, and a titanium kitchen. It is, of course, already rented by someone else. You will never rent this apartment. You'll be lucky to get invited to a party there, where everyone will be dressed better than you, and you'll stand around drinking overpriced vodka, thinking about how you will never live like this.

The perfect apartment deal, on the other hand, is theoretically attainable. It is that brilliant coup lurking in the crevices of the market, a mysteriously cheap but eminently livable place that everyone else has somehow missed. I believed firmly in its existence, a belief fueled partly by persistent rumors of fabulous, underpriced apartments locked into rent-controlled prices now found only in Little Rock and Omaha. Since the late 1990s, San Franciscans have passed around such rental urban legends at parties as bits of real estate gossip.

"Did I tell you about my boyfriend's friend who has a four-hundred-dollar studio in Pacific Heights?" a recent acquaintance would tell me as we stood crushed together holding plastic cups in an overcrowded kitchen. "It was handed down to her from a guy she met at the taqueria."

Such tales always lacked some crucial identifying feature, some clue as to how I, too, might find my own bed/bath bargain. I don't recall ever seeing those party talkers again or visiting any of their friends' friend's apartments. But the stories were enough to maintain my dream that, if I just searched long enough, hidden gems awaited.

So it was, working in my overpriced home office one morning, on perhaps my second or third daily turn through Craigslist, I saw it:

$1,450 / 2 br–1 bath near Duboce Park

The listing at first seemed too implausible to accept. Finding a two-bedroom apartment for that price, in a decent neighborhood in San Francisco, was roughly the equivalent of a metal detector–wielding beachcomber finding a jewel-encrusted crown buried in the sand. It's possible, of course, but when your giant headphones go beep, you can probably assume it's just a stray quarter. I suspected that the apartment had been mislabeled—as listings often purposely are—but the body of the ad very clearly noted two bedrooms. There was more: "wood floors, back deck, city views." And then the neighborhood! Lloyd Street, where the apartment purportedly existed, is a quaint one-block alley a few blocks from my current apartment. Duboce Park—which many people call Dog Shit Park, for obvious reasons, but which is still one of the city's best locations for observing its bizarre dog-owner subculture—was my neighborhood park. I called the number for the property management agency and set up an appointment to see it that afternoon.

• • •

If there is one rule that nearly always holds for apartment searching in a city like San Francisco, it is that listings that sound too good to be true, are. In fact, listings that sound crappy are usually too good to be true. There are certain coded phrases by which a seasoned Craigslister can detect a whiff of deception: "cute" (translation: small), "cozy" (tiny), "nice paint" (otherwise run-down), "great price" (total shithole). Any attribute listed in ALL CAPS and framed by exclamation points means the apartment is being oversold. A landlord who schedules an open house of only fifteen minutes is likely to be even more anal and irritating than the average landlord, which is to say two standard deviations more anal and irritating than the general population. Yet even the most experienced apartment hunter will end up visiting five to ten places that have some laughable shortcoming—a studio with no windows, perhaps, or a bathroom shared with a family of six next door and an owner straight-facedly offering it for $1,000 a month.

The Lloyd Street listing contained no obvious trickery, but nonetheless I started with the assumption that the apartment contained a horrible disfiguring secret. I walked over to Lloyd Street and found a four-apartment building at the top of a steep hill. John, the rental agent, pulled up on time in a standard-issue rental agency sedan and climbed out, wearing the standard-issue rental agency gear of a button-down shirt over khakis. He shook my hand and took me up to the second floor.

At first glance, the place (fig. 1) appeared less than new, yet not significantly dilapidated. The layout was fairly typical of San Francisco railroad flats, with a long hallway connecting two bedrooms—one quite large, with a city view, one medium-size—in the front to the kitchen in the back, with a small living room in between. There were reasonably high ceilings, and wood floors that were worn but passable. It had a large kitchen, one of the few I'd seen that actually qualified as "eat-in," and beyond that was an enclosed laundry porch and bathroom. Off the laundry porch was a deck

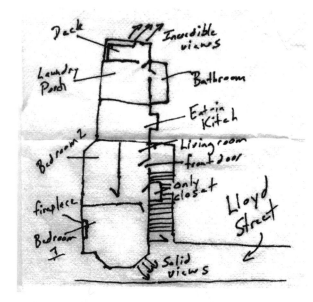

Fig. 1

which, perched on the back side of the steep hill, had one of the most strik-ing downtown and bay views I'd seen in the city.

By all appearances there was nothing amiss with the place and, starting with the views, there were a lot of positive features. That such an apartment would be listed at $1,450, then, made no sense. I had per-sonally viewed dank basement two-bedrooms for which the landlords were seeking—and got—$2,000 or more. So something had to be wrong, and I walked through again with an eye trained for flaws. I noted a single closet in the hall, which would mean acquiring some kind of wardrobes for the bedrooms. The living room was also fairly narrow, the light fixtures were a little beat-up, and the paint was peeling in several places. The kitchen appliances were dated. Still, it didn't add up. A hint of hope began to germinate that I had actually stumbled upon, if not the perfect apartment deal, then a close approximation of it.

Unlike the pushy agents I regularly encountered, who followed me around pointing out claw-footed tubs and cozy closet/bedrooms, John had politely left me alone while I looked at the place. I found him at the front door and confronted him directly. "Is this listing right? This place is $1,450?" I asked, showing him the printout to make sure there would be no confusion.

"Mmm-hmm, yes," he said in a half mumble, half whisper that forced me to lean in close to hear him. When I leaned toward him, however, he stepped back, necessitating that I step toward him and lean in farther.

"Per month?" I said, backing him toward the door.

"Mmm-hmm."

"Is there something wrong with it?"

"What do you mean? Mmm, no, don't think so."

"Do you know what two bedrooms go for in this city?"

"Well, I'm just the agent," he mumble-whispered. "The owners have rented it out for years. When the last tenant moved out they just told me to rent it at the same price. And by the way," he said offhand-edly, "mmm, I'm going to have them paint the whole thing, put in new light fixtures, and new appliances in the kitchen."

New appliances in the kitchen? Done and done. This was it, the perfect apartment deal. The scenario was exactly as I had dreamed it would be: Some hippy out-of-town landlord, probably living at a Zen center in Marin County and unaware of the gross inflation in the market over the past decade, was still trying to get his 1990 rent. I felt my pocket for my checkbook, which I always carried to apartment viewings for just such an occasion. No need to be rash, though, better to be sure. I wandered back to reinspect the laundry porch, with John tailing along. I asked him if he would be installing a washer and dryer, or if I would have to get my own.

"Mmm, no," he said. "You can't put a washer and dryer in here. This is an old laundry porch, but I don't think they want it used for that now."

This was, potentially, a disaster. I coveted laundry like no other apartment feature, so much so that a washer/dryer was perhaps the number one crucial element of the perfect apartment deal. Every time I hauled a month-and-a-half's worth of clothing down my stairs and five blocks up the hill to the Laundromat, I swore that my next home would include a washer/dryer. Each year for Christmas I asked family members for two things only: socks and underwear, thereby upping my laundry-limiting factor annually until finally I could hold out long enough to produce more laundry than I could carry. A washer and dryer in my apartment would change all that, and would be a step up in the world, a rare move on my part in the direction of maturity and refinement. Making a quick calculation, I determined that the Laundromat was actually three blocks farther from Lloyd Street than my current apartment. "Are you sure they won't let me put one in?" I asked, whiny desperation seeping into my voice.

"Ummm, I can ask them," he said.

"Please," I said, taking a rental application from his pile. I filled it out and gave it to him, and asked him to hold it until he heard about the laundry.

The other day I read that the median price for a single family home in San Francisco has now risen above $600,000. This is the latest in a long string of bad news, of course, for anyone hoping to buy a home in the city or anywhere closer to it than the soul-killing suburbs an hour's commute away. On the other hand, the ever-rising prices have the advantage of providing the basis for 60 to 80 percent of all conversation among those renters who lack any reasonable hope of buying. People with no interest in real estate at all, after living for just a few weeks in San Francisco, will find themselves drawn to the topic the very moment a conversation lulls. "Yeah, I love the Bay Area, but I'll just never be able to afford to buy. . . . It's a trade-off, you know? It's such a great city, but . . . I just don't know who's buying all these houses. . . . We looked at some places last weekend, just ridiculous. . . . There's always Oakland. . . . Even that's too expensive now. Even *Oakland!*"

When I first moved to San Francisco after college, I—like many who end up here—lived in a basement room that was roughly the size of a double bed, with a breadbox closet and a street-level window looking out onto the interstate exit ramp. I had five roommates, a moderate-to-serious rodent problem, and an insane landlord/slumlord whose legions of non-English-speaking repairmen showed up at all hours to explain, using hand gestures, that they couldn't fix whatever was broken that day. Those were happy times, though, not least because there was never a shortage of things to complain about. Most people I know in San Francisco, especially those who arrived during the dot-com boom and (like me) found no way to profit from it, are bound together by similar experiences. Many of us, now in our late twenties or early thirties, still live with roommates, whether out of choice or continuing financial necessity. (During the last mayoral election, many such people even touted the thirtysomething Green party candidate's living with roommates as a sign that he remained, in some only-in-San Francisco sense, "a man of the people." He lost a close election to a man of the same age who lived, in a less populist manner, with his wife.)

Others, like myself at the time of the Lloyd Street find, had chosen to commit every extra penny toward living alone. (For me the decision to sacrifice financial well-being for living conditions was rooted in a desire—since lost—to create an appearance of stability. Plus, I neither had anyone to live with nor the energy to locate strangers.) Those, really, were and remain the only two options. But the Lloyd Street apartment offered an enviable third way. I could pay a little more than I was already shelling out and have an entire extra bedroom (not to mention the deck, the eat-in, the views) all to myself. Or, I could find a roommate and pay, by San Francisco standards, an absurdly reasonable split rent. On the other hand, however, was the fact that moving was always a pain in the ass, with hidden expenses and lost deposit monies. The easiest thing to do vis-à-vis Lloyd Street, I decided, was to let laundry decide the matter.

The day after I saw the apartment, John called back to tell me that the owners were inflexible on the laundry issue. They were, it seemed, irrationally terrified of water damage. The call was a crushing blow that threw me into a further state of indecision. I asked John if I could see the apartment once more, and he met me there again the following day. This time I stood for several minutes in each room, soaking in the atmosphere of the place. I sat on the deck and looked out over the city, waiting for an impulse, a spark of conviction that would carry me over the threshold. After a while John seemed to be getting antsy, so I thanked him and walked back home.

From that point on, I thought about the apartment almost constantly, unable to choose. I polled my friends and family members, describing the layout and drawing it on napkins. I placed every combination of financial calculations into a spreadsheet, printed it out, and stared at it. I doubled and trebled my Craigslist searching, comparing listings to the Lloyd Street benchmark. I even returned to the apartment several times, examining the building from the outside and testing the walk to the Laundromat. At one point I saw a painter go in and convinced him to let me come up with him and look again. I quizzed him on his opinion of the place, but he didn't speak much English and just shrugged his shoulders.

"Why don't you just take it?" my girlfriend said, after I had spent an entire dinner dissecting the issue for her. She had a stake in the outcome of the decision, of course. But more than that, she had a stake in the decision being made, so that I would stop talking about it. I explained again about the lack of laundry. "Fine, then," she said, "don't take it." I complained that she was just telling me what I wanted to hear.

Then, one morning after several days of this, I got a call from John. "Mmm, yes, about that Lloyd Street apartment," he said. My heart sank. I knew he was going to tell me it was taken. Why had I waited? In that moment, the very moment that it was already too late, I firmly decided that I wanted it.

"The owner has decided to lower the rent to $1,375," he said. "There hasn't been that much interest in it." Lowered? No interest? Impossible! But here was John, mumbling it to me over the phone. The new price was a mere $25 more than my current apartment. Now the place was mine, and my indecision had won me $75 a month.

But wait, what did all of those uninterested people know that I didn't? Why were people looking at this apartment and not taking it? I lost my nerve. I hedged. "I'll have to think about it some more," I said. "I'll call you tomorrow."

The next morning I awoke to a voice mail from John. "Mmm, I just wanted to let you know that I have another renter for the Lloyd Street apartment," he said. "But, he needs a cosigner, and you had your application in first. If you want it, it's yours. Let me know today."

Finally, the truly decisive moment had come. Was it the perfect apartment deal or not? I thought about hauling my laundry to the Laundromat. I thought about the many wise people who had passed over the apartment, detecting fatal flaws that I had overlooked. I called John and turned it down. He seemed a little surprised; he asked me if I was sure. I was, I told him. It just wasn't for me. Maybe with a washer/dryer, I said, it would have been worth the move.

• • •

I felt a little wistful about it, but only in the sense that the perfect apartment deal had been ruined by its lack of laundry. Overall I was confident with my decision. Then, after a couple hours had passed, I happened to look over at my closet, overflowing with a waist-high pile of clothes. A thought dawned on me: I was paying $1,350 a month to not have laundry *right now.* Not taking the apartment had failed to improve my laundry situation. I had passed up what was now quite clearly the ultimate once-in-a-lifetime apartment deal, for laundry that I didn't have anyway.

I rummaged through my recycling bin and found a crumpled printout of the listing. I called the agency. John wasn't there, so I told the sunny-sounding woman who picked up the phone about my situation, about having turned down one of John's apartments that morning and now wanting it back.

"Oh, you mean the place on Lloyd Street?" she asked.

"Yes! That's the one. Lloyd Street."

"Oooo, I'm sorry. Someone just signed the lease an hour ago. But if that falls through, we'll be sure to give you a call."

When I hung up the phone, I felt that familiar pain in my stomach, the knot of regret common to the chronically indecisive. I routinely experienced this emotion upon hearing that a girlfriend I had broken up with had found a new serious boyfriend, or seeing people excelling in jobs I had passed up, or deciding on a burrito for dinner instead of a falafel. It was a feeling triggered by the realization that doors of possibility—whether for the reconciliation of a long-ended relationship or for tonight's dinner—were being closed forever, combined with the suspicion that I had sacrificed something sublime in the name of seeking something better. Twenties life offered an endless array of possibilities of where to live, who to date, what to do with oneself, but it was the plague of possibilities that seemed to often render me completely paralyzed, unable to make any decision at all. The dilemma was always when to give up *the good* in order to hold out for *the perfect.* Just as Craigslist was full of apartments waiting to be discovered, viewed, considered, so too was the world full of new romances to be attempted, career changes in waiting, and corners of the planet left unexplored and un-lived-in.

Pondering all this, I realized that I'd been wrong to think that Lloyd Street would have been the perfect apartment if only it had contained laundry. The truth was that there was no perfect apartment deal; the Shangri-la I was searching for didn't exist. Holding out for perfection was just a rationalization for refusing to accept that reality lacks easy answers, and that only a fantasy life is devoid of compromises. It's an excuse to always push the prospect of real contentment around the next corner, or in my case, to the next hour's search of Craigslist.

Figuring out the error in my thinking, however, was no excuse for accepting mediocrity in my current situation. So a couple months after giving up Lloyd Street, I moved out of my own apartment and went traveling.

It's been two years now since I found and gave up the perfect apartment deal. I'm back in San Francisco. I still think about the place whenever I walk by Lloyd Street, which happens roughly once a week. I stopped spending much time on Craigslist afterward, though; lightning never strikes twice and all that. I have moved a couple times, and now I live in a nice remodeled place down the hill from Lloyd, with congenial landlords and its own washer/dryer. The rent is $1,880 a month, which of course I split with my roommate.

I kept John's number, however, and each time I move I call him up to ask about the Lloyd Street apartment. "Mmm, sorry," he says quietly, "it's not available." Once he offered to show me another place, a two-bedroom a couple blocks down the street, which he was offering for $1,650. As the market here goes, the price was a steal. I looked at it. But it sucked, just as I'd suspected it would.

ROOMMATE PET PEEVES

- Demanding that we rotate who pays for the stamps on bills.

- Having sex in the bunk bed above me, assuming I was asleep. I wasn't.

- Creating a spreadsheet for me and the other roommate to track what time we turned the air-conditioning on and off, so that she could bill us for it.

- Not restocking the toilet paper, even when I go to the extreme measure of hiding my own stash in the hope that they will *have* to buy the next supply.

- Leaving nasty hairballs in the shower drain (especially if you live with seven other girls).

- Not holding up his end of the bargain. When the toilet seat broke, I made a deal with my roommate: I would take on the embarrassing task of buying a toilet seat if he'd stock up on toilet paper. He showed up with a pathetic four-pack (I was thinking along the lines of a mondo twenty-four-pack), so I bought a forest green squishy grandma toilet seat in retaliation.

- Modifying the toilet by attaching a kitchen sink sprayer that would operate as a homemade bidet.

- Refusing to pay rent. When the other roommates and I told her that she needed to pay rent or move out, she called 9-1-1 and told the police that we were harassing her. An officer came to our house and gave us little domestic violence pamphlets.

- Writing initials on everything he owned—even the Kleenex box.

- Bringing random wastoids home with her. In the middle of the night I went to the kitchen to get a drink of water, only to be completely freaked out by an extremely intoxicated guy—wearing only leopard print bikini underwear—who got lost trying to find his way back to my roomie's room. Guys like this were such a problem that I started chaining my mountain bike to our kitchen radiator.

- Gutting a deer on the kitchen floor. (I lived in Montana.)

- Lying pathologically. My roommate had me naively believing that the magazine pictures on the wall were of her model boyfriend. For six months I empathetically listened to hours of fake relationship problems.

IN MY TRIBE

by Ethan Watters

You may be like me: between the ages of 25 and 39, single, a college-educated city dweller. If so, you may have also had the unpleasant experience of discovering that you have been identified (by the U.S. Census Bureau, no less) as one of the fastest-growing groups in America—the "never marrieds." In less than 30 years, the number of never-marrieds has more than doubled, apparently pushing back the median age of marriage to the oldest it has been in our country's history—about 25 years for women and 27 for men.

As if the connotation of "never married" weren't negative enough, the vilification of our group has been swift and shrill. These statistics prove a "titanic loss of family values," according to *The Washington Times*. An article in *Time* magazine asked whether "picky" women were "denying themselves and society the benefits of marriage" and in the process kicking off "an outbreak of 'Sex and the City' promiscuity." In a study on marriage conducted at Rutgers University, researchers say the "social glue" of the family is at stake, adding ominously that "crime rates . . . are highly correlated with a large percentage of unmarried young males."

Although I never planned it, I can tell you how I became a never-married. Thirteen years ago, I moved to San Francisco for what I assumed was a brief transition period between college and marriage. The problem was, I wasn't just looking for an appropriate spouse. To use the language of the Rutgers researchers, I was "soul-mate searching." Like 94 percent of never-marrieds from 20 to 29, I, too, agree with the statement "When you marry, you want your spouse to be your soul mate first and foremost." This *über*-romantic view is something new. In a 1965 survey, fully three out of four college women said they'd marry a man they didn't love if he fit their criteria in every other way. I discovered along with my friends that finding that soul mate wasn't easy. Girlfriends came and went, as did jobs and apartments. The constant in my life—by default, not by plan—became a loose group of friends. After a few years, that group's membership and routines began to solidify. We met weekly for dinner at a neighborhood restaurant. We traveled together, moved one another's furniture, painted one another's apartments, cheered one another on at sporting events and open-mike nights. One day I discovered that the transition period I thought I was living wasn't a transition period at all. Something real and important had grown there. I belonged to an urban tribe.

I use the word "tribe" quite literally here: this is a tight group, with unspoken roles and hierarchies, whose members think of each other as "us" and the rest of the world as "them." This bond is clearest in times of trouble. After earthquakes (or the recent terrorist strikes), my instinct to huddle with and protect my group is no different from what I'd feel for my family.

Once I identified this in my own life, I began to see tribes everywhere I looked: a house of ex-sorority women in Philadelphia, a team of ultimate-frisbee players in Boston, and groups of musicians in Austin, Texas. Cities, I've come to believe, aren't emotional wastelands where fragile individuals with arrested development mope around self-indulgently searching for true love. There are rich landscapes filled with urban tribes.

So what does it mean that we've quietly added the tribe years as a developmental stage to adulthood? Because our friends in the tribe hold us responsible for our actions, I doubt it will mean a wild swing toward promiscuity or crime. Tribal behavior does not prove a loss of "family values." It is a fresh expression of them.

It is true, though, that marriage and the tribe are at odds. As many ex-girlfriends will ruefully tell you, loyalty to the tribe can wreak havoc on romantic relationships. Not surprisingly, marriage usually signals the beginning of the end of tribal membership. From inside the group, marriage can seem like a risky gambit. When members of our tribe choose to get married, the rest of us talk about them with grave concern, as if they've joined a religion that requires them to live in a guarded compound.

But we also know that the urban tribe can't exist forever. Those of us who have entered our mid-30s find ourselves feeling vaguely as if we're living in the latter episodes of "Seinfeld" or "Friends," as if the plot lines of our lives have begun to wear thin.

So, although tribe membership may delay marriage, that is where most of us are still heading. And it turns out there may be some good news when we get there. Divorce rates have leveled off. Tim Heaton, a sociologist at Brigham Young University, says he believes he knows why. He argues that it is because people are getting married later.

Could it be that we who have been biding our time in happy tribes are now actually grown up enough to understand what we need in a mate? What a fantastic twist—we "never marrieds" may end up revitalizing the very institution we've supposedly been undermining.

And there's another dynamic worth considering. Those of us who find it so hard to leave our tribes will not choose marriage blithely, as if it is the inevitable next step in our lives, the way middle-class high-school kids choose college. When we go to the altar, we will be sacrificing something precious. In that sacrifice, we may begin to learn to treat our marriages with the reverence they need to survive.

BUDGET RECIPES

Microwave S'Mores

Serving size: 1 s'more

Ingredients:
1 tsp. peanut butter
2 saltine crackers
1 large marshmallow

The basic idea:
1. Spread peanut butter on one side of both crackers.
2. Sandwich marshmallow between crackers.
3. Microwave for approximately 5–10 seconds—keep an eye on the marshmallow and stop as soon as it puffs up (if you don't cook it long enough, the marshmallow stays raw, but if you cook it too long, the marshmallow gets tough).
4. Eat immediately, being careful not to burn your tongue on hot sugary goo.
5. Repeat as necessary.

Five-Minute Key Lime Pie

Serving size: 1 pie

Ingredients:
Juice from 4–5 limes (about 1 cup) and grated rind from
    those limes (about 1 tbsp.)
1 can (8 oz.) sweetend condensed milk
premade graham cracker pie shell

The basic idea:
1. Stir lime rinds and lime juice into condensed milk.
2. Pour mixture into pie shell.
3. Refrigerate for two hours.
4. Serve and enjoy.

Redeem Your Ramen: Ramen Plus!

Serving size: 1 bowl

Ingredients:
1 package ramen noodles
Any vegetables on hand (broccoli, spinach, asparagus, etc.)
Tofu, cut into squares (optional)

The basic idea:
1. Cook noodles according to package directions.
2. Two minutes before noodles are fully cooked, add chopped
    vegetables and tofu.
3. Stir and serve hot for a nearly nutritious meal!

PEOPLE LIKE YOU

by Sarah Eisenstein

After attempted eye contact and communication with all my other new neighbors had failed, I met Roger almost too easily, by engaging in the kind of awkward small talk that advice columnists suggest to people who have never made a friend.

"Sure is hot outside for April," I said. When he smiled and fanned himself in agreement, I felt bolder. "Lived here long?" I asked.

"My whole life," he said, and his words made my heart race like love.

When I met Roger, I had been living in a massive apartment building in Flatbush, Brooklyn, for a little more than a year. Talking with friends from other New York neighborhoods, I would often find a way to smugly insert how much I pay in rent ($468 a month!—dirt cheap for New York) into conversation. Not to mention the fact that my building looks directly onto Prospect Park and is located across from an express train to Manhattan. Besides the rent and location, you can buy fresh coconut and sugar cane on the corner in the summer. My block also has a drum circle, a Caribbean market, and a table of elderly ladies with a sign that says ALL YOUR BIBLE QUESTIONS ANSWERED HERE.

But in a place where everybody seemed to greet each other as "Brother This" or "Sister That," I felt disconnected and invisible, not to mention guilty of gentrifying the neighborhood. Normally, I was so busy trying to figure out what my new neighbors thought of me *(Do they hate me?)* that I could barely even smile at them and say hello.

But here I was—actually making conversation with a lifer—and things felt different. "Wow!" I said. "You've lived here your whole life."

Roger was clearly encouraged by my positive response as well. "I could tell you everything about the building, the neighborhood. Come by my apartment some time, I live in 4A."

"I will *definitely* do that," I said.

By this time we were outside, and going in separate directions. "See you later," I said, waving, as I stepped into a flawless spring day in the park.

In seventh grade, due to what must have been a case of pity or mistaken identity, I got invited to Rebekah Maschiano's exclusive birthday party. Thinking about my brief conversation with Roger, I felt like I had that invitation in my hand again. I had my ticket, and oh, would I ride. Now that I knew Roger, I would meet other people in the neighborhood. Casual greetings would abound. Maybe someone would even ask me, "How ya doin', Sister?"

Then the sound of someone running up behind me and yelling my name shook me out of my reverie. Roger's sweatband had slipped over one eye. He was breathing heavily. "When are you coming over?" he said.

I had been hoping to meet someone a little *less* desperate than myself, not the other way around. Still, a lifer was a lifer. "Oh, maybe I could drop by on Wednesday?" I said.

"What time on Wednesday?" he insisted.

"Oh, maybe noonish," I said casually.

"Okay, just don't forget," he said.

• • •

"You're late," Roger said as he opened the door. "You were supposed to come at noon. I thought maybe you wouldn't come. I was
really hoping you wouldn't stand me up. You wouldn't stand me up,
would you?"

Any leftover excitement I had about this little get-together quickly
drained away. "Roger, what are you talking about? I'm here. I'm only
fifteen minutes late." How was I on the defensive with someone I didn't
even know? Roger was a big guy, and now that it appeared he didn't
hang out with reality much, the idea of entering his apartment alone
was making me a little nervous. "I need to walk to the library," I said. "Do
you want to walk to the library with me?"

He agreed, but on the stairs he got upset again. "You said you
would be here at noon, and you weren't."

When he finally calmed down, our walk got a little better, and we
did discover a little common ground (he had gotten lost in Prospect
Park too; people in the building think he's a narc and don't like him).
Then he asked me if I had a boyfriend.

The only thing I manage to bring up in conversation more often
than my low rent is the fact that I'm gay. I will tell construction workers who whistle at me on the street that I have a girlfriend. Last week I
tried to come out to a group of my students who don't yet speak
English. Of course, I immediately told Roger that I'm gay.

Unlike my students, who probably assumed they had the wrong
pronouns, Roger responded immediately and strongly. "Damn, you're a
homo!" he shouted. "I can't believe it. You're a homo!" I had already
noticed his habit of popping the air with his fist and saying *"Bam!"* —
the whole homo revelation prompted him to do it twice.

Any normal person would have aborted our trip and insisted on
walking to the library by herself at this point. Instead, I said, "Roger,

you're being homophobic, and that makes me not want to hang out with you."

Chastened, he assured me, "I really like lesbians, if ya know what I mean. It's just dudes bangin' each other. Damn, gross!" He made a face normally associated with vomiting.

"Roger, you know, usually when guys hate gay men it's because they're threatened. Maybe you're gay. Have you ever thought about that?"

"Oh, somebody says I'm a homo, and *bam!*" He popped his fist into the air with even more force.

Slightly shaken, I decided to change the subject. I had never been so relieved to see the grand fake-Greek facade of the Brooklyn Public Library rise into view.

I told Roger that I needed to use the computer, so he walked me most of the way to the Internet alcove. We paused to say our good-byes. "So can I come over sometime?" he said.

"I guess so, maybe."

"Do you think your girlfriend would mind?"

"Why would my girlfriend mind?" I said. "You're my neighbor, you might drop by."

"So she wouldn't mind if we're like . . ." Here, he made an unsubtle gesture with his pelvis. "Ooh, maybe she'd like to get in on it." A grin crept across his pudgy face. The father half of a father-son combo get-ting a drink at the water fountain was trying to pretend not to stare; the son stared openly.

"Roger, we will not be like . . . we will not be anything, because there is *nothing between us*," I said. The father gave up trying and stared along with his son. "I will be going to use the computers now, and you will not come with me," I said to Roger, illustrating my half of the deal by strid-ing intentionally over to the computer section. I didn't look back.

• • •

Why had I tried so hard with Roger? Sure, it would have been nice to have a friend in the building. But my self-esteem has improved measurably since seventh grade. I'm not that excited to get invited to birthday parties anymore. And I didn't care about my neighbors that much when I lived in swanky Park Slope. Was I just having a BlackPeopleLikeUs.com moment, needing to be the cool white girl accepted by my black neighbors?

I had another encounter with Roger a few weeks later, when I was helping a new roommate move in. We were lounging in the stairwell, getting ready to try to shove a couch in the door, when Roger walked by. I introduced them and mentioned that Roger was our upstairs neighbor, when he offered his first bit of insight. "This neighborhood sucks. But now that white people like you are moving in, it's better." Funny, that's what Jimmy from building management had implied when he put my new roommate on the lease, saying, "We really want more people *like you* in the building."

People like you: young, white, professional. Transient enough so that rent control doesn't become too bothersome (the management company is allowed to jack up the rent when we move out), and stable/professional-looking/white enough to attract the people who will pay even higher rents. Beyond a simple desire for acceptance, my desperation to fit in was driven by the need to be more than just another *person like me.*

I recently ran into an acquaintance named Betsy on my way home, and when she found out where I live, she asked, "Do you feel safe there?" I shrugged and said I hadn't had any problems, to which she responded, "Oh, but isn't it a little bit . . . *ghetto?*" She paused before the word "ghetto," waiting for me to agree before she had to say it.

"I guess it depends on what you mean by 'ghetto,'" I said coldly. But I knew exactly what Betsy was talking about. At that moment I could have admitted that I've gripped my keys like a weapon in anticipatory self-defense. That I do my shopping in other neighborhoods because the milk on the shelves here is minutes from its expiration date. But I was in a self-righteous groove. I kept walking, but a little bit farther away from her, just to make my disapproval clear.

"I used to live in Crown Heights," Betsy said quickly.

Please shut up, I thought. "Yeah?" I said.

"My girlfriend and I were part of this wave of young, middle-class white dykes gentrifying the neighborhood," she said, "and we just felt like our neighbors resented us."

"My building has a tenants' association, so that probably helps," I said. It is true that one of the longtime residents in my building organized a tenants' meeting last winter, after our landlord "forgot" to pay the heating bill for the third time. It is not strictly true to say that we have a tenants' association, since our third meeting was supposed to be four months ago. Still, the heat did get turned back on.

"Oh," Betsy said, finally giving in to the overwhelming force of my self-righteousness. "Well, I used to live there, but we found it too, you know, difficult, I guess."

Yup. Sure. It's one thing to displace people. And it's a whole other thing to turn around and blame them for how bad it makes us feel. Agreeing felt too much like complicity, so I just shrugged and kept on walking.

PARENTS ARE THE NEW FRIENDS

by Rachel Hutton

"I learned a new word," Mom calls from the other room. *"Bauchle,"* she says. "It's Scottish." It sounds like an herbal remedy, something like ginkgo biloba. I peek into the living room, where she's sitting in a dark green recliner, cocked halfway back, reading the newspaper.

"What's it mean?" I ask, approaching the chair. I lean my head over her shoulder, infringing on her personal space like I did in the womb.

"A shabby or worn-out shoe," she says. "It can also be applied to people." Mom eyes my outfit. I want to protest, but instead I laugh. I am wearing a faded hoodie sweatshirt, fleece pajama pants, and a pair of old sneakers. My hair is pulled up in a messy fan, strands falling in every direction. I am twenty-eight years old, and I live with my parents.

This is the third time since I graduated from college that my parents have welcomed me back home: first, when I returned to Minneapolis after two years in New York; next, after my roommates went off to graduate school; and finally, now, telling people I gave up my apartment because I wanted to save money for an extended trip abroad, though I'm not really sure if that's true.

I have to have a *reason*, though. I can't just say, "I live with my parents," and leave it hanging in the air as if the sentence had ended with "my boyfriend" or "my friend." It's the raised eyebrows and quizzical looks that make me quickly follow up with a "because" when news of my domestic situation slips out. Usually, I avoid the question, making only general statements about where I reside. When pressed, I answer, almost too casually, "Yeah, I have a couple of roommates."

When confronted with the thought of moving home, most of my peers wouldn't consider it. Having last night's hot hookup run into Mom and Dad at the breakfast table? And where would I keep my "stash"? For some, the deal breaker is the loss of independence, which can feel like outright suffocation. (One of my friends says that when he visits his parents for the holidays, they follow him from room to room.) Regressing to your old self—the one with the oversize glasses and feathered hair staring back from the frame on your parents' bureau—seems too much to bear.

But let's be honest—even when I had my own apartment, the last three guys I brought home were all on the covers of magazines. And the last time I smoked weed was, well . . . never. (In college I dreamed of working for the FBI.)

Of course, there is that nagging sense of defeat, of having struck out on your own only to have, well, struck out. Do others think I'm the prim spinster, doting on her ailing mother, cross-stitching the evening away? Or am I like the guy holed up in the basement since high school, lying on his back listening to Pink Floyd, working a pizza delivery job, trying to "find himself"?

In reality, I am neither. A couple of times I picked up and moved halfway across the country. First San Francisco, then New York. Each time starting over: navigating unknown cities, getting jobs, finding apartments, making new friends, and, yes, inevitably "finding myself."

So by choosing to return to the past, to live with people who have been known to drive "ugly" cars (the brown station wagon) or wear "weird" clothes (a grungy Old Style beer T-shirt), or say embarrassing things in front of my friends (oh, there are so many . . .), I risk dropping to the bottom of the social ladder.

Here's the real reason I moved back in with my parents: Despite the relative unhipness of the situation, the remoteness of our suburban location, and my frustrations with chicken knickknacks and a quarter-century's worth of accumulation in the basement, if I could pick any roommates in town—Prince, Josh Hartnett, Garrison Keillor—I would choose my parents. I don't mean to insult my friends, but look who they're competing with. What kind of roommate offers to drive you to the airport at 4 a.m.? Or stays by your side if you have the flu? Who else, frankly, would let you room rent-free?

Still, we have our separate lives. Sometimes we are close strangers, hours and hours spent traversing the same space, each with our own agenda. I come home late from work, microwave a plate of leftovers, and sit down to read a magazine; Mom talks on the phone with her sister; Dad watches the ten o'clock news. It's like sitting in a freeway traffic jam and looking through the glass at all the neatly packaged drivers. But then, out of the mundane puttering of everyday life, as my mother swallows her evening regimen of pills before shuffling off to bed, she will say something about my character or my dreams. Something offhand, yet prescient, and I will remember: *Of course you know. . . . I am half of you.*

My mom doesn't think I've overstayed my welcome. In fact, when she tells other people I live with them, she lets them know it's not a chore. "It's like we have our own personal chef," she adds generously, though at home she'll mock-whine, "You're always trying to feed us tofu."

• • •

When I was a child, I didn't see my parents as anything beyond their roles as Mom and Dad. It was like the way I viewed my grade school teachers until the first time I saw Ms. Jensen at the grocery store, and realized—*gasp*—she had a life outside of school. Now as an adult, I'm gaining a better understanding of my parents' other selves: as husband, wife, sibling, son, employee, employer, and friend. I watch my dad open a stack of mail, hoping the checks exceed the bills. My mom picks out a card for him, and I wonder about the message she'll write.

In between the daily routine, I hear more stories from their pasts: Dad growing up in rural Minnesota, driving a tractor as a six-year-old, working his way through law school, Mom teaching kindergarten, sharing a tiny apartment with her friend, being rescued from a knife-wielding attacker by a college boyfriend.

If I had visited my parents only sporadically over the past decade, they'd probably still be the caricatures of my youth, those same security guards preventing me from exploring life's more interesting fringes. Because I am spending time with them, day in and day out, their lives take on more nuance and shape. My brother, in California, knows only the outline of what's happening, bullet points over a phone line. But in a facial expression or a catch in the voice, I see their vulnerability, and their pride.

I watch my parents cycle through their lives, some arcs high, others low. Some of the moments are weighty and wide: crying beside my great-aunt's casket, yelling until the other leaves the house. Others are the tiny details of human days: ironing shirts; standing in front of the refrigerator with the door open; falling asleep by the TV, mouth open, remote clenched.

As the three of us get older, the social gap between us narrows to a slit. We'll go on a bike ride, or go out to brunch, or pop a batch of popcorn and watch *Desperate Housewives* (though I pretend not to understand some of the jokes so I don't have to explain the innuendoes). I take my mom to a film opening, and she sashays around in gold slippers, blending in with the hipster crowd. Soon I'm tagging along to a sixtysomething dinner party, knocking back a few Manhattans. I lift my glass as if to toast: *Some say friends are the new family; I say parents are the new friends.*

My dad has suggested he and my mother go to a movie, so he stands at the kitchen table, helplessly rifling through a pile of newspapers, as if he has just arrived in this country and doesn't understand the moviegoing procedure.

"Which section am I supposed to look in?" he asks, frustrated.

"Variety," my mom calls from the living room. I grab Variety and open it to the movie listings page. My dad reaches for his pocket and puts on his glasses.

"You're sixty years old and you don't know how to find a movie?" I ask.

"That's what I have a wife for," he responds, mostly—but not completely—joking.

"You need to set a better example," I say, pointing a finger. "Because if this is what husbands are like, I don't want one—and then I'll be living with you guys forever."

As much as I love living with my parents, my stay with them will be temporary. The problem with our getting along so well is that there's less incentive for me to seek out others my age. And while in the short-term, my de facto dating hiatus is not a big deal (yes, an ex-boyfriend, visiting from out of town, stayed overnight with the three of us), ultimately it's the crux of the matter. Although maybe I'll never get it—so I risk losing face by admitting this—I want the same companionship that I see in my parents' partnership. If I want my own such relationship someday, I know I must first take leave of theirs.

"SO . . . ARE YOU TWO TOGETHER?"

by Pagan Kennedy

Liz is explaining the situation to some guy in customer service. "My roommate and I need to network our computers together," she's saying, seated at the other desk in the office that we share.

The word "roommate" jumps out at me. It's an inadequate word, but it's all we have. What else do you call two friends who are shacked up together in a decaying Victorian, run several businesses and one nonprofit group out of its rooms, host political meetings under oil portraits of Puritan and Jewish ancestors, cook kale and tofu meals for all who stop by, go to parties as a couple, and spend holidays with each other's families? If we were lesbians—as people sometimes assume us to be—we would fit more neatly into a box. But we're straight.

In the year and a half we've lived together, I have struggled with the namelessness of our situation. The word "roommate" conjures up a college dorm, scuff marks on the floors from hundreds of anonymous occupants, locks on all the doors, the refrigerator Balkanized into zones where you can or cannot put your food, Death Metal blasting from the speakers down the hall. It means transience and 20 years old. It does not mean love or family.

Words offer shelter. They help love stay. I wish for a word that two friends could live inside, like a shingled house with faded Persian rugs. Sometimes, in an attempt to make our relationship sound more valid, I tell people Liz and I are in a "Boston marriage." The usual response is, "You're in a what?"

It's an antique phrase, dating back to the 1800s. In Victorian times, women who wanted to maintain their independence and freedom opted out of marriage and often paired up to live together, acting as each other's "wives" and "helpmeets." Henry James's 1886 novel about such a liaison, *The Bostonians*, may have been the inspiration for the term, or perhaps it was the most glamorous female couples who made their homes in Boston, including Sarah Orne Jewett, a novelist, and her "wife" Annie Adams Fields, also a writer.

Were they gay? Was the "Boston marriage" simply a code word for lesbian love? Historian Lillian Faderman says this is impossible to determine, because nineteenth-century women who kept diaries drew curtains over their bedroom windows. They did not bother to mention whether their ecstatic friendship spilled over into—as Faderman so romantically puts it—"genital sex." And ladies, especially well-to-do ones who poured tea with their pinkies raised, were presumed to have no sex drive at all. Women could share a bed, nuzzle in public, and make eyes at each other, and these cooings were considered to be as innocent as schoolgirl crushes.

So, at least in theory, the Boston marriage indicated a platonic, albeit nerdy relationship. With ink-stained fingers, the Victorian roommate-friends would smear jam on thick slices of bread and then lounge across from each other in bohemian-shabby leather armchairs to discuss a novel-in-progress or a political speech they'd just drafted. Their brains beat as passionately as their hearts. The arrangement often became less a marriage than a commune of two, complete with a political agenda and lesson plan.

"We will work at [learning German] together—we will study every-thing," proposes Olive, a character in *The Bostonians*, to her ladylove. Olive imagines them enjoying "still winter evenings under the lamp, with falling snow outside, and tea on a little table, and successful ren-derings . . . of Goethe, almost the only foreign author she cared about; for she hated the writing of the French, in spite of the importance they have given to women." James poked fun at Olive's bookworm passion. But he lavished praise on his own sister Alice's intense and committed friendship with another woman, which he considered to be pure, a perfect devotion.

Most likely, the Boston marriage was many things to many women: business partnership, artistic collaboration, lesbian romance. And some-times it was a friendship nurtured with all the care that we usually squan-der on our mates—a friendship as it could be if we made it the center of our lives.

"I am on my way through the green lane to meet you, and my heart goes scampering so, that I have much ado to bring it back again, and learn it to be patient, till that dear Susie comes," Emily Dickinson wrote to her friend—and maybe lover—Sue Gilbert. Today I see tragedy in these words, for Sue ended up married to Emily's brother, and the women never had a chance to build a life around their love. I find myself wishing I could teleport them to our own time, so that Emily D. and her Susie might find an apartment in San Francisco together, fly a rainbow flag out front, shop at Good Vibrations, and delight one another with dildos in shocking shades of pink. And yet, it's not that simple. When I read the passionate letters between nineteenth-century women, I become keenly aware of what I'm miss-ing, of how much richer Victorian friendships must have been. While our sex lives have ballooned in the last hundred years, our friendships have grown stunted. Why don't I shower my favorite girls with kisses and "mash" notes, hold hands with them as we skip down the street, or share a sleeping bag? We don't touch anymore. We don't dare admit how our hearts scamper.

Several years ago, I fell in love with a man because of all he carried—he would show up for the night with five plastic bags rattling on his arm, and then proceed to unpack, strewing possessions everywhere. The next day, I'd find his orange juice in the refrigerator, his sweater tucked into my bureau, a new software program installed on my computer. Night after night, he installed himself in my apartment.

At first, every one of these discoveries charmed me—his way of saying, "I need to be with you." But one morning, I surveyed my bedroom—guy's underwear on the floor, books about artificial intelligence stacked on the night table, a jar of protein powder on the shelf—and realized that I had a live-in boyfriend. And that he and I had completely different ideas about what we wanted from a living space. He thought of an apartment as a desktop where we could scatter papers, coffee mugs, and computer parts. What I regarded as a mess, he saw as a filing system that should under no circumstances be disturbed. Meanwhile, I drove him crazy by hosting political meetings in our living room, inviting ten people over for dinner at the last minute. We loved one another, but that didn't mean we should share an apartment.

And then—when our Felix-Oscar dynamic seemed insurmountable—I picked up a magazine called *Maxine* and stumbled across an article that gripped me. Written by 27-year-old Zoe Zolbrod, it celebrated the passion that flashes up between women, even when they are both straight: "I would meet women who I would need to know with an urgency so crushing it gave the crush its name. And in knowing them I would feel a rush of power and possibility, of total self, that seemed much more real to me than heterolove," Zolbrod wrote. When she met her friend V, "it was like finding the person you think you'll marry." The two moved in together. They took care of each other, became family, called each other "my love" and "my roommate" interchangeably.

I remember reading that article and thinking, "yes." I adored my boyfriend, but he and I had never meshed in the way that Zolbrod described. We tried to make a home together, but we didn't agree on what a home should be.

Years later, when our love fizzled into friendship and he moved out, I made a vow to myself: I would not drift into a domestic situation again. Instead, I would find someone who shared my passion for turning a house into a community center—with expansive meals, weekend guests, clean counters, flowers, art projects, activist gatherings, a backyard garden, and a pile of old bikes on the porch, available to anyone needing to borrow some wheels.

My friend Liz seemed like the right person. And so I proposed to her. Did she want to be a co-creator of the performance art piece that we would call "home"? She did.

Recently, at a party, I met a thirtysomething academic who has settled alone in a small town outside of Boston. "I can step right out my door and cross-country ski," she told me. "But I'm lonely a lot." Around us, people sweated and threw their arms wildly in time to an old Prince song. The academic wedged her hands into her jeans pockets, and her eyes skated past my face and scanned the room.

If you're lonely, get a roommate, I suggested. Move into a group house. "No," she sighed. "I'm too old for that. I'm set in my ways." What if you marry? I asked. She laughed. "That's different."

She might be speaking for thousands, millions of women all over this country. According to the U.S. Census Bureau, one out of four households in 1995 had only one member, a figure expected to rise sharply as the population ages. I see the future of single women, and frankly, it depresses the hell out of me. We're isolating ourselves in condos and studio apartments. And why? Sometimes because we need to bask in solitude—and that's fine. But other times, it's because we're afraid to get too comfortable with our friends. What if you bought a house with your best friend, opened a joint bank account with her, raised a child? Where would your bedmate fit into the scheme? This is where the platonic marriage—for all its loveliness—may force you to make some difficult choices and rethink your ideas about commitment.

Liz's love, a theoretical physicist, meanders down our street clapping. Standing beside a triple-decker house, he cocks his head, listening to the sharp sounds reverberating off of a vinyl-sided wall. He's designing an exercise for the students in the "Physics of Music" class that he's assistant-teaching. When he's done, he'll come back inside to find Liz and me draped across the sofa, discussing urban sprawl. We'll all make dinner together, and if I feel like it, I might join them for a night out, or I might head off with the guy that I'm seeing.

I date scientists too, men who understand what it is to experiment, to question and wonder. Liz's love or mine might sit in our kitchen scrawling equations into a notebook, or disappear for days to orbit with subatomic particles or speak with machines. These men are wise enough to see that the Boston marriage works to their advantage. Liz and I keep each other company. Our Boston marriage has made it easier for us to enjoy the men in our lives.

But how do we commit to each other, knowing that someday one of us may marry? One of us might fall in love with something other than a man—a solar cabin in Mexico, a job in Tangier, a documentary film project in Florida, a year of silence in the Berkshire woods. Any number of things could pull us apart. We have made no promises to each other, signed no agreements to commit. For some reason, that seems O.K. most of the time.

For this article, I talked to many women who'd formed platonic marriages or who'd thought about it seriously. All of them discussed the complicated issues of commitment, or lack thereof, between friends.

Janet calls her arrangement with Greta intentional. "In the same vein as creating an 'intentional community,' we have an 'intentional' living arrangement," she says. The two high school friends, both straight women in their early thirties, moved to Boston together five years ago, knowing that they would share an apartment, and a life. They eat dinner together and check in with the how-was-your-day conversation most people expect from a mate.

"Greta is the person I say to contact when I fill out emergency cards," Janet tells me. "She is the first person I would turn to if I needed help."

And yet, the two have left their future open, and the promises they have made to each other are full of what-ifs. If Greta doesn't marry by the time she's 35, they might raise a child together. It's the what-ifs that drive many women away from closeness with each other.

One married woman, I'll call her Lisa, says she's deeply disappointed with the way women treat their friendships as disposable, dumping friends when an erotic partner comes along. "Even though my friends and I used to talk about buying a house together, we all knew at some level that it wasn't going to work. Ultimately, we would betray each other, find a man, marry him. I got married because I knew everybody else was going to. If I knew I could trust a friendship with a woman—that there was a way of making a friendship into a bona fide, future-oriented relationship—I would rather have that than be married."

As for me, I've come to think of commitment as something beyond a marriage contract, a joint bank account, or even a shared child. I know that eventually Liz and I may drift to other houses, other cities. Yet I can picture us reuniting at age 80, to settle down in an old-age home together. Maybe we will have husbands, maybe not, but we'll still be conspirators. We'll probably harangue the youngsters who spoon spinach onto our plates about the importance of forming a union; we'll attend protests with signs duct-taped to our walkers; maybe we'll write an opera and perform it using some newfangled technology that lets us float in the air. Liz and I are committed. We share a vision of the kind of people we want to be and the world we want to inhabit.

"We formed a family core with the possibility of exhilaration," wrote Zoe Zolbrod in her article. "Yet Hallmark never even named a goddamn holiday after us, can you believe it?" We're not sure what to call ourselves. We have no holidays. We don't know what our future holds. We have only love and the story we are making up together.

Liz sashays into the kitchen, a shopping bag crinkling under her arm. "I bought you these," she says, "because you've been wearing those mismatched gloves with holes in them."

I slide on the mittens, and my hands turn into fuzzy paws, pink and red with a touch of gold. "I love them," I say, and hug her, patting her back with my fuzz. She laughs and shifts her eyes away, a bit embarrassed by her own generosity. "I couldn't have my roommate going around in shabby gloves," she says.

She uses the word "roommate." But I know what she means.

THE FLING,

THE DISASTER,

"THE ONE"

TAKING OFF

by Davy Rothbart

Some folks fall in love gradually; for me it always happens in an instant. I was at the airport in Albuquerque, headed for California, when I saw a beautiful girl dressed in white, maybe twenty-three years old. I watched her at the check-in counter—she was sad but radiant, and she moved and spoke delicately, like an Arctic bird on a fragile bit of ice. She was accompanied by an oafish guy in a hot pink NO FEAR T-shirt, who was pestering the lady behind the counter with questions about the plane: Was it a 747 or a 767? The lady had no idea, but he was determined to pry an answer from her. It seemed inconceivable that this guy was that girl's boyfriend, and yet, the world is filled with strangeness.

After they finished at the counter, they said their good-byes and—to my delight—headed off separately. I was startled to see that the girl walked with a slow, struggling flop-leggedness, as though both her knees were made of rubber, an exaggerated kind of limp. This effortful gait combined with her sad glow twisted something in me; my heart hurt, and I was in love.

It's been my peculiar blessing that every time I see a beautiful girl in an airport, she ends up sitting next to me on the plane. This has led

to a number of thrilling flights filled with animated conversation followed by an exchange of e-mail addresses at baggage claim. There was
Imogina, the young scientist on the flight from Bogotá to Miami, who
was coming to the U.S. for the first time to study domesticated birds;
Alexandra, on the red-eye from San Francisco to Baltimore, who was
making a documentary film about competitive jump-roping; Krystal,
on the short hop from Cincinnati to Little Rock, who was headed home
from her parents' funeral (they'd crashed their motorcycle in the rain).
But what do you e-mail to a girl who lives in Jacksonville or Vancouver
or Dublin who you'll probably never see again? Ships cross once and
again—it never adds up to much.

So it was no surprise, but a kind of painful wonder, when I got on
the plane in Albuquerque and found myself sharing a row with the
flop-legged girl in white. She had the window, I had the aisle. Between
us, her purse and my backpack shared a seat.

Our plane rocketed into the sky and the girl looked forlornly out
the window. I waited for her to glance my way so I could begin the
conversation that I guessed would awkwardly end when we parted
ways in San Diego. But she was so lost in her aching thoughts that
she never turned from the window, even when the beverage cart
rolled past with pretzels and Cokes. To busy myself, and because it
was the only other thing on my mind, I reached into my bag and
retrieved a printout of the short story I'd just finished that morning.
I went through it, making little changes, turning the pages loudly in
hopes that the girl would peek over. It hurt to have her so close and
inattentive. Her lips were pursed; her eyes cut at the clouds. In a
way, she was too nicely dressed for my taste—in the kind of little
white tennis dress a girl might don for a late brunch in the
Hamptons—but that bland elegance felt exotic and made me hunger
for her more.

I looked back at the typed pages in my hands—I was still in that fleeting honeymoon phase you'll sometimes have with a just-finished story, where for a moment everything about it feels perfect and snugly in place. Finally I said to the girl, "Hey, what's your name?"

She smiled at me, which was a surprise. Her name was Kara. She was a student in Seattle. I asked about her boyfriend's interest in planes. "Boyfriend?" "At the check-in." "Oh, no," she explained, that was only her cousin; she'd been visiting family in New Mexico. I'd thought her melancholy would make conversation lurch and buckle, but everything sailed smooth as could be—she acted oddly grateful for the small talk, and she seemed to occasionally hold my gaze for an extra sixteenth note. But how could I parlay this chance meeting and warm chemistry into a lasting love?

I told Kara I'd be right back and took the riddle with me to the back of the plane. I stretched my legs and listened to two male flight attendants tease each other about some misadventure involving a motorcycle and a birthday gift. My emotions whooshed and flared like Independence Day rockets. I was panicked, sick, desperate with longing. It had been a long time since I'd had a true love in my life, and it seemed to me that meeting a girl on an airplane would be a serendipitous way to break out of a four-season slump.

I needed to give Kara something that would keep us in contact, but what? A few mini bottles of liquor? No, she was too high-class to get drunk on airplane vodka. One of the little Delta blankets, snatched from an overhead compartment? I imagined the look she'd give me, a pained patience usually reserved for dealing with deranged street preachers. Then I knew at once—I'd give her the story. It would communicate something of me, and more important, it would give her something to respond to, a reason to stay in touch. I glided back down the aisle and took my seat again. Kara laughed, "Wondered if you were coming back."

"Got held up in traffic," I said. "Listen, do you like to read?"

"What?"

"Reading, do you like to read?"

She paused and thought about it. Granted, it was a stupid question, but not a complicated one. At last she said, "No."

"No? You don't like to read?"

"No," she said. "I hate reading."

"You hate reading."

"I just don't like it."

"You just don't like it." I laughed. She clearly wasn't kidding. All I could do was repeat after her like an idiot child.

"Sometimes I read magazines," she offered hopefully.

"Sometimes you read magazines."

"But only sometimes. Mostly I look at the cosmetics."

Sadly, shamefully, pathetically, I forced my story on her anyway. I tried to explain what it was about, but the crashing down of my fantasies made me tongue-tied and weary. I wrote my e-mail address and cell phone number at the top. "In case you want to let me know what you thought of it," I said.

Kara smiled brightly and folded the story carefully into her purse, as though it were a sick mouse. Later, I imagined, she'd rid herself of the thing in the ladies' room trash can.

In San Diego I was headed for baggage claim and she was off to catch her connecting flight. We hugged. She had no scent at all. I knew—for that reason, somehow—that I would never hear from her. "Keep in touch," I said.

"I will," she said. Then her face took on the dark look she'd had when I'd first seen her. She turned, and I stood watching as she shuffled away down the long corridor, until at last she disappeared out of sight. I felt stunned and blasted, like a little kid thrown from his bicycle into the hard dirt. People brushed past me on all sides, hurrying to catch flights, make calls, grab newspapers, or find their luggage, and I bounced around in their wake.

ON THE FRINGES OF THE PHYSICAL WORLD

by Meghan Daum

It started in cold weather; fall was drifting away into an intolerable chill. I was on the tail end of twenty-six, living in New York City, and trying to support myself as a writer. One morning I logged on to my America Online account to find a message under the heading "is this the real meghan daum?" It came from someone with the screen name PFSlider. The body of the message consisted of five sentences, written entirely in lowercase letters, of perfectly turned flattery, something about PFSlider's admiration of some newspaper and magazine articles I had published over the last year and a half, something else about his resulting infatuation with me, and something about his being a sportswriter in California.

I was charmed for a moment or so, engaged for the thirty seconds that it took me to read the message and fashion a reply. Though it felt strange to be in the position of confirming that I was indeed "the real meghan daum," I managed to say, "Yes, it's me. Thank you for writing." I clicked the "Send Now" icon and shot my words into the void, where I forgot about PFSlider until the next day when I received another message, this one entitled "eureka." "wow, it is you," he wrote, still in lowercase. He chronicled the various conditions under which he'd read my few and far between articles: a boardwalk in Laguna Beach, the spring training pressroom for the baseball team he covered for a Los Angeles newspaper. He confessed to having a "crazy crush" on me. He referred to me as "princess daum." He said he wanted to propose marriage or at least have lunch with me during one of his two annual trips to New York. He managed to do all of this without sounding like a schmuck. As I read the note, I smiled the kind of smile one tries to suppress, the kind of smile that arises during a sappy movie one never even admits to seeing. The letter was outrageous and endearingly pathetic, possibly the practical joke of a friend trying to rouse me out of a temporary writer's block. But the kindness pouring forth from my computer screen was unprecedented and bizarrely exhilarating. I logged off and thought about it for a few hours before writing back to express how flattered and touched—this was probably the first time I had ever used the word "touched" in earnest—I was by his message.

I had received e-mail messages from strangers before, most of them kind and friendly and courteous—all of those qualities that generally get checked with the coats at the cocktail parties that comprise what the information age has now forced us to call the "three-dimensional world." I am always warmed by an unsolicited gesture of admiration or encouragement, amazed that anyone would bother, shocked that communication from a stranger could be fueled by anything other than an attempt to get a job or make what the professional world has come to call "a connection."

I am not what most people would call a "computer person." I have utterly no interest in chat rooms, news groups, or most Web sites. I derive a palpable thrill from sticking an actual letter in the U.S. mail. But e-mail, though at that time I generally only sent and received a few messages a week, proves a useful forum for my particular communication anxieties. I have a constant, low-grade fear of the telephone. I often call people with the intention of getting their answering machines. There is something about the live voice that has become startling, unnervingly organic, as volatile as incendiary talk radio. PFSlider and I tossed a few innocuous, smart-assed notes back and forth over the week following his first message. His name was Pete. He was twenty-nine and single. I revealed very little about myself, relying instead on the ironic commentary and forced witticisms that are the conceit of most e-mail messages. But I quickly developed an oblique affection for PFSlider. I was excited when there was a message from him, mildly depressed when there wasn't. After a few weeks, he gave me his phone number. I did not give him mine but he looked me up anyway and called me one Friday night. I was home. I picked up the phone. His voice was jarring yet not unpleasant. He held up more than his end of the conversation for an hour, and when he asked permission to call me again, I accepted as though we were in a previous century.

Pete, as I was forced to call him on the phone—I never could wrap my mind around his actual name, privately referring to him as PFSlider, "e-mail guy," or even "baseball boy"—began calling me two or three times a week. He asked if he could meet me in person and I said that would be okay. Christmas was a few weeks away and he would be returning east to see his family. From there, he would take the short flight to New York and have lunch with me. "It is my off-season mission to meet you," he said. "There will probably be a snowstorm," I said. "I'll take a team of sled dogs," he answered. We talked about our work and our families, about baseball and Bill Clinton and Howard Stern and sex, about his hatred for Los Angeles and how much he wanted a new job. Other times we would find each other logged on to America Online at the same time and type back and forth for hours. For me, this was far superior to the phone. Through typos and misspellings, he flirted maniacally. "I have an absurd crush on you," he said. "If I like you in person you must promise to marry me." I was coy and conceited, telling him to get a life, baiting him into complimenting me further, teasing him in a way I would never have dared in the real world or even on the phone. I would stay up until 3 a.m. typing with him, smiling at the screen, getting so giddy that I couldn't fall asleep. I was having difficulty recalling what I used to do at night. My phone was tied up for hours at a time. No one in the real world could reach me, and I didn't really care.

In off moments, I heard echoes of things I'd said just weeks earlier: "The Internet is destroying the world. Human communication will be rendered obsolete. We will all develop carpal tunnel syndrome and die." But curiously, the Internet, at least in the limited form in which I was using it, was having the opposite effect. My interaction with PFSlider was more human than much of what I experienced in the day-light realm of live beings. I was certainly putting more energy into the relationship than I had put into any before, giving him attention that was by definition undivided, relishing the safety of the distance by opting to be truthful rather than doling out the white lies that have become the staple of real life. The outside world—the place where I walked around on the concrete, avoiding people I didn't want to deal with, peppering the ground with half-truths, and applying my motto of "let the machine take it" to almost any scenario—was sliding into the periphery of my mind. I was a better person with PFSlider. I was some-one I could live with.

This borrowed identity is, of course, the primary convention of Internet relationships. The false comfort of the cyberspace persona has been identified as one of the maladies of our time, another avenue for the remoteness that so famously plagues contemporary life. But the better person that I was to PFSlider was not a result of being a differ-ent person to him. It was simply that I was a desired person, the object of a blind man's gaze. I may not have known my suitor, but for the first time in my life, I knew the deal. I knew when I'd hear from him and how I'd hear from him. I knew he wanted me because he said he wanted me, because the distance and facelessness and lack of gravity of it all allowed him to be sweeter to me than most real-life people had ever managed. For the first time in my life, I was involved in a ritualized courtship. Never before had I realized how much that kind of structure was missing from my everyday life.

And so PFSlider became my everyday life. All the tangible stuff— the trees outside, my friends, the weather—fell away. I could physically feel my brain. My body did not exist. I had no skin, no hair, no bones; all desire had converted itself into a cerebral current that reached nothing but my frontal lobe. Lust was something not felt but thought. My brain was devouring all of my other organs and gaining speed with each swallow. There was no outdoors, the sky and wind were irrelevant. There was only the computer screen and the phone, my chair and maybe a glass of water. Pete started calling every day, sometimes twice, even three times. Most mornings I would wake up to find a message from PFSlider, composed in Pacific time while I slept in the wee hours. "I had a date last night," he wrote, "and I am not ashamed to say it was doomed from the start because I couldn't stop thinking about you." Then, a few days later, "If you stood before me now, I would plant the warmest kiss on your cheek that I could muster."

I fired back a message slapping his hand. "We must be careful where we tread," I said. This was true but not sincere. I wanted it, all of it. I wanted the deepest bow down before me. I wanted my ego not merely massaged but kneaded. I wanted unfettered affection, soul mating, true romance. In the weeks that had elapsed since I picked up "is this the real meghan daum?" the real me underwent some kind of meltdown, a systemic rejection of all the savvy and independence I had worn for years like a grown-up Girl Scout badge. Since graduating from college, I had spent three years in a serious relationship and two years in a state of neither looking for a boyfriend nor particularly avoiding one. I had had the requisite number of false starts and five-night stands, dates that I wasn't sure were dates, emphatically casual affairs that buckled under their own inertia even before dawn broke through the iron-guarded windows of stale, one-room city apartments. Even though I was heading into my late twenties, I was still a child, ignorant of dance steps or health insurance, a prisoner of credit-card debt and student loans and the nagging feeling that I didn't want anyone to find me until I had pulled myself into some semblance of an adult. I was a true believer in the urban dream—in years of struggle succumbing to brilliant success, in getting a break, in making it. Like most of my friends, I was selfish by design. To want was more virtuous than to need. I wanted someone to love me but I certainly didn't need it. I didn't want to be alone, but as long as I was, I had no choice but to wear my solitude as though it were haute couture. The worst sin imaginable was not cruelty or bitchiness or even professional failure but vulnerability. To admit to loneliness was to slap the face of progress. It was to betray the times in which we lived.

But PFSlider derailed me. He gave me all of what I'd never realized I wanted. He called not only when he said he would, but unexpectedly, just to say hello. His guard was not merely down but nonexistent. He let his phone bill grow to towering proportions. He thought about me all the time and admitted it. He talked about me with his friends and admitted it. He arranged his holiday schedule around our impending date. He managed to charm me with sports analogies. He courted and wooed and romanced me. He didn't hesitate. He was unblinking and unapologetic, all nerviness and balls to the wall. He wasn't cheap. He went out of his way. I'd never seen anything like it.

Of all the troubling details of this story, the one that bothers me the most is the way I slurped up his attention like some kind of dying animal. My addiction to PFSlider's messages indicated a monstrous narcissism. But it also revealed a subtler desire that I didn't fully understand at the time. My need to experience an old-fashioned kind of courtship was stronger than I had ever imagined. The epistolary quality of our relationship put our communication closer to the eighteenth century than the uncertain millennium. For the first time in my life, I was not involved in a protracted "hang out" that would lead to a quasi-romance. I was involved in a well-defined structure, a neat little space in which we were both safe to express the panic and intrigue of our mutual affection. Our interaction was refreshingly orderly, noble in its vigor, dignified despite its shamelessness. It was far removed from the randomness of real-life relationships. We had an intimacy that seemed custom-made for our strange, lonely times. It seemed custom-made for me.

The day of our date was frigid and sunny. Pete was sitting at the bar of the restaurant when I arrived. We shook hands. For a split second he leaned toward me with his chin as if to kiss me. He was shorter than I had imagined, though he was not short. He registered to me as neither handsome nor un-handsome. He had very nice hands. He wore a very nice shirt. We were seated at a very nice table. I scanned the restaurant for people I knew, saw no one and couldn't decide how I felt about that.

He talked and I heard nothing he said. He talked and talked and talked. I stared at his profile and tried to figure out if I liked him. He seemed to be saying nothing in particular, though it went on forever. Later we went to the Museum of Natural History and watched a science film about the physics of storms. We walked around looking for the dinosaurs and he talked so much that I wanted to cry. Outside, walking along Central Park West at dusk, through the leaves, past the horse-drawn carriages and yellow cabs and splendid lights of Manhattan at Christmas, he grabbed my hand to kiss me and I didn't let him. I felt as if my brain had been stuffed with cotton. Then, for some reason, I invited him back to my apartment, gave him a few beers, and finally let him kiss me on the lumpy futon in my bedroom. The radiator clanked. The phone rang and the machine picked up. A car alarm blared outside. A key turned in the door as one of my roommates came home. I had no sensation at all, only the dull déjà vu of being back in some college dorm room, making out in a generic fashion on an Indian throw rug while Cat Stevens' *Greatest Hits* played on the portable stereo. I wanted Pete out of my apartment. I wanted to hand him his coat, close the door behind him, and fight the ensuing emptiness by turning on the computer and taking comfort in PFSlider.

When Pete finally did leave, I sulked. The ax had fallen. He'd talked way too much. He was hyper. He hadn't let me talk, although I hadn't tried very hard. I berated myself from every angle, for not kissing him on Central Park West, for letting him kiss me at all, for not liking him, for wanting to like him more than I had wanted anything in such a long time. I was horrified by the realization that I had invested so heavily in a made-up character, a character in whose creation I'd had a greater hand than even Pete himself. How could I, a person so self-congratulatingly reasonable, have gotten sucked into a scenario that was more akin to a television talk show than the relatively full and sophisticated life I was so convinced I led? How could I have received a fan letter and allowed it to go this far? Then a huge bouquet of FTD flowers arrived from him. No one had ever sent me flowers before. I was sick with sadness. I hated either the world or myself, and probably both.

No one had ever forced me to forgive them before. But for some reason, I forgave Pete. I cut him more slack than I ever had anyone. I granted him an official pardon, excused his failure for not living up to PFSlider. Instead of blaming him, I blamed the Earth itself, the invasion of tangible things into the immaculate communication PFSlider and I had created. With its roommates and ringing phones and sub-zero temperatures, the physical world came barreling in with all the obstreperousness of a major weather system, and I ignored it. As human beings with actual flesh and hand gestures and Gap clothing, Pete and I were utterly incompatible, but I pretended otherwise. In the weeks that followed I pictured him and saw the image of a plane lifting off over an overcast city. PFSlider was otherworldly, more a concept than a person. His romance lay in the notion of flight, the physics of gravity defiance. So when he offered to send me a plane ticket to spend the weekend with him in Los Angeles, I took it as an extension of our blissful remoteness, a three-dimensional e-mail message lasting an entire weekend. I pretended it was a good idea.

The temperature on the runway at JFK was seven degrees Fahrenheit. We sat for three hours waiting for de-icing. Finally we took off over the frozen city, the DC-10 hurling itself against the wind. The ground below shrank into a drawing of itself. Laptop computers were plopped onto tray tables. The air recirculated and dried out my contact lenses. I watched movies without the sound and thought to myself that they were probably better that way. Something about the plastic interior of the fuselage and the plastic forks and the din of the air and the engines was soothing and strangely sexy, as fabricated and seductive as PFSlider. I thought about Pete and wondered if I could ever turn him into an actual human being, if I could ever even want to. I knew so many people in real life, people to whom I spoke face-to-face, people who made me laugh or made me frustrated or happy or bored. But I'd never given any of them as much as I'd given PFSlider. I'd never forgiven their spasms and their

speeches, never tied up my phone for hours in order to talk to them. I'd
never bestowed such senseless tenderness on anyone.

We descended into LAX. We hit the tarmac and the seat belt signs
blinked off. I hadn't moved my body in eight hours, and now, I was
walking through the tunnel to the gate, my clothes wrinkled, my hair
matted, my hands shaking. When I saw Pete in the terminal, his face
registered to me as blank and impossible to process as the first time I'd
met him. He kissed me chastely. On the way out to the parking lot, he
told me that he was being seriously considered for a job in New York.
He was flying back there next week. If he got the job he'd be moving
within the month. I looked at him in astonishment. Something silent
and invisible seemed to fall on us. Outside, the wind was warm and the
Avis and Hertz buses ambled alongside the curb of Terminal 5. The
palm trees shook and the air seemed as heavy and earthly as Pete's
hand, which held mine for a few seconds before dropping it to get his
car keys out of his pocket. The leaves on the trees were unmanageably
real. He stood before me, all flesh and preoccupation. The physical
world had invaded our space. For this I could not forgive him.

Everything now was for the touching. Everything was buildings and
bushes, parking meters and screen doors and sofas. Gone was the computer; the erotic darkness of the telephone; the clean, single dimension
of Pete's voice at 1 a.m. It was nighttime, yet the combination of sight
and sound was blinding. We went to a restaurant and ate outside on the
sidewalk. We were strained for conversation. I tried not to care. We
drove to his apartment and stood under the ceiling light not really
looking at each other. Something was happening that we needed to
snap out of. Any moment now, I thought. Any moment and we'll be all
right. These moments were crowded with elements, with carpet fibers
and direct light and the smells of everything that had a smell. They left
marks as they passed. It was all wrong. Gravity was all there was.

For three days, we crawled along the ground and tried to pull our-selves up. We talked about things that I can no longer remember. We read the *Los Angeles Times* over breakfast. We drove north past Santa Barbara to tour the wine country. I stomped around in my clunky shoes and black leather jacket, a killer of ants and earthworms and any hope in our abilities to speak and be understood. Not until studying myself in the bathroom mirror of a highway rest stop did I fully realize the preposterousness of my uniform. I felt like the shot in a human shot put, an object that could not be lifted, something that secretly weighed more than the world itself. We ate an expensive dinner. We checked into a hotel and watched television. Pete talked at me and through me and past me. I tried to listen. I tried to talk. But I bored myself and irritated him. Our conversation was a needle that could not be threaded. Still, we played nice. We tried to care and pretended to keep trying long after we had given up. In the car on the way home, he told me I was cynical, and I didn't have the presence of mind to ask him just how many cynics he had met who would travel three thousand miles to see someone they barely knew. Just for a chance. Just because the depths of my hope exceeded the thickness of my leather jacket and the thickness of my skin. And at that moment, I released myself into the sharp knowledge that communication had once again eliminated itself as a possibility.

Pete drove me to the airport at 7 a.m. so I could make my eight o'clock flight home. He kissed me goodbye, another chaste peck I rec-ognized from countless dinner parties and dud dates from real life. He said he'd call me in a few days when he got to New York for his job interview, which we had discussed only in passing and with no refer-ence to the fact that New York was where I happened to live. I returned home to the frozen January. A few days later, he came to New York and we didn't see each other. He called me from the plane back to Los

Angeles to tell me, through the static, that he had gotten the job. He was moving to my city.

PFSlider was dead. Pete had killed him. I had killed him. I'd killed my own persona too, the girl on the phone and online, the character created by some writer who'd captured him one morning long ago as he read the newspaper. There would be no meeting him in distant hotel lobbies during the baseball season. There would be no more phone calls or e-mail messages. In a single moment, Pete had completed his journey out of our mating dance and officially stepped into the regular world, the world that gnawed at me daily, the world that fed those five-night stands, the world where romance could not be sustained because we simply did not know how to do it. Here, we were all chitchat and leather jackets, bold proclaimers of all that we did not need. But what struck me most about this affair was the unpredictable nature of our demise. Unlike most cyber romances, which seem to come fully equipped with the inevitable set of misrepresentations and false expectations, PFSlider and I had played it fairly straight. Neither of us had lied. We'd done the best we could. We were dead from natural causes rather than virtual ones.

Within a two-week period after I returned from Los Angeles, at least seven people confessed to me the vagaries of their own e-mail affairs. This topic arose, unprompted, over the course of normal conversation. Four of these people had gotten on planes and met their correspondents, traveling from New Haven to Baltimore, New York to Montana, Texas to Virginia, and New York to Johannesburg. These were normal people, writers and lawyers and scientists, whom I knew from the real world. They were all smart, attractive, and more than a little sheepish about admitting just how deep they had been sucked in. Very few had met in chat rooms. Instead, the messages had started after chance meetings at parties and on planes; some, like me, had received notes in response to things they'd written online or elsewhere. Two of these people had fallen in love, the others chalked it up to a strange, uniquely postmodern experience. They all did things they would never do in the real world: they sent flowers, they took chances, they forgave. I heard most of these stories in the close confines of smoky bars and crowded restaurants, and we would all shake our heads in bewilderment as we told our tales, our eyes focused on some distant point that could never be reigned in to the surface of the Earth. Mostly it was the courtship ritual that had drawn us in. We had finally wooed and been wooed, given an old-fashioned structure through which to attempt the process of romance. E-mail had become an electronic epistle, a yearned-for rule book. The black and white of the type, the welcome respite from the distractions of smells and weather and other people, had, in effect, allowed us to be vulnerable and passionate enough to actually care about something. It allowed us to do what was necessary to experience love. It was not the Internet that contributed to our remote, fragmented lives. The problem was life itself.

The story of PFSlider still makes me sad. Not so much because we no longer have anything to do with one another, but because it forces me to grapple with all three dimensions of daily life with greater awareness than I used to. After it became clear that our relationship would never transcend the screen and the phone, after the painful realization that our face-to-face knowledge of each other had in fact permanently contaminated the screen and the phone, I hit the pavement again, went through the motions of real life, said "hello" and "goodbye" to people in the regular way. In darker moments, I remain mortified by everything that happened with PFSlider. It terrifies me to admit to a firsthand understanding of the way the heart and the ego are entwined. Like diseased trees that have folded in on one another, our need to worship fuses with our need to be worshipped. Love eventually becomes only about how much mystique can be maintained. It upsets me even more to see how this entanglement is made so much more intense, so unhampered and intoxicating, by way of a remote access like e-mail. But I'm also thankful that I was forced to unpack the raw truth of my need and stare at it for a while. This was a dare I wouldn't have taken in three dimensions.

The last time I saw Pete he was in New York, thousands of miles away from what had been his home and a million miles away from PFSlider. In a final gesture of decency, in what I later realized was the most ordinary kind of closure, he took me out to dinner. We talked about nothing. He paid the bill. He drove me home in his rental car, the smell and sound of which was as arbitrary and impersonal as what we now were to each other. Then he disappeared forever. He became part of the muddy earth, as unmysterious as anything located next door. I stood on my stoop and felt that familiar rush of indifference. Pete had joined the angry and exhausted living. He drifted into my chaos, and joined me down in reality where, even if we met on the street, we'd never see each other again, our faces obscured by the branches and bodies and falling debris that make up the ether of the physical world.

FAKE DATING

by Tim Gihring

On my most recent, and final, fake date, we dressed as though for a wedding: suit and tie for me, little black dress for her. We danced, we drank, we whispered wisecracks. We amused each other, we showed off. We made an effort, and complimented each other for it. It was a night when I thought that she, at twenty-six, and I, at thirty-one, had grown into ourselves completely, a night when I noticed that her eyes were inky mirrors of the evening sky, petroleum pools dotted with diamonds. But it was no one's wedding, and certainly—most absolutely—not ours. It was an orchestra concert, and I had free tickets. When, at one point, she dropped on bended knee—her short, shiny black hair flipping aggressively forward—and said, "Will you marry me?" I laughed instead of cried; I may even have yawned. As midnight rolled around, she dropped me at my apartment, and after promises to talk soon, we went our separate ways, the moon finished its rounds, and no one felt the need to lasso it for anyone.

At the concert people buzzed, "Aren't you the cute couple?" They said, "You're a good dancer, and so is your lover." And we smiled. No one needed to know: It was fake. Not fake like one of us was fooling the other, being disingenuous, being a dick, as though halfway through the risotto I'd change into pajamas, brandish some Cracker Jack, and whip out a Game Boy—*Sorry, you thought this was a date?* Nor was it arrested development, playing at being adults. It was neither of these things, and yet, in a way, it was both. It was fake dating. It was what I did last year.

I hardly invented fake dating. It was once a sad synonym for the kind of outing where one person puckers for a good-night smooch on the porch and the other is halfway into the house. But to make that scenario a foregone conclusion—to deliberately embark on a fake date—is a new evolution. Fake dating is saying, let's get to know each other better without even expecting that good-night smack. It's saying, in this day and age of the three-date rule, let's have a preseason.

We should have seen it coming. Because we're crazy now. We're crazy self-conscious (thanks, ad industry), we're crazy self-absorbed (thanks, pop psychology), we're crazy obsessed with finding fault (thanks, talk radio), and we're just plain crazy crazy (thanks, bovine growth hormone). Today the idea that we could be crazy about a person sounds, well, crazy. Without trotting out the well-known divorce statistics, let's just say we've upped the ante on romantic expectations while simultaneously expecting to be disappointed. Fake dating begins to look rational.

Many people meet their spouses either in college or soon after. So, for those entering their thirties more unattached than the day they were born, dating is—while frequently better than in younger years— something definitely different. There may be a long string of failed romances, even divorce, within our own pasts and those of the people we meet. Close friendships within intimate circles may be more fulfilling, more honest, and more progressive than troublesome relationships. Is a fake date any more fake, really, than what transpires on a "real" date? If we consider our motives, biological or otherwise, who are we really fooling with the flattery and flowers? (We all know, of course, what flowers demand of bees.)

On that final fake date, we didn't exactly go our separate ways, alone to separate beds. I went to mine, all right, and she to hers, but hers may not have been empty. She has a boyfriend. This I knew. In a way, this made it the ultimate fake date. It wasn't the windup to anything, it just was: fun and unencumbered, without momentum— momentary. Inertia is underrated. You may enjoy yourself more when you're not concerned with where things are going. Of course, inertia can also be frustrating. The true test of a fake date is whether you're happy to leave when your date disappears into her house, and the door, which was never really open, closes in your face. I sometimes caught myself with a foot in the door.

Our final fake date was the last of many. She was not my only fake date, but she was the first. We started fake dating because there are only two things to do when you meet someone already committed— move on or try to move them onto you—and we wanted a third choice. When I met her and got to know her, I found her attractive. Slim, dark, and quiet, she was someone you wanted to wisk to Tangier, place in a café with strong drinks and weak ceiling fans, and meet all over again. Hers was not a mystery you could walk away from—you had to run or stay. I chose the latter. My friends thought I was crazy. But because of that decision, I learned a new kind of relationship. I could let her know I found her attractive, as a compliment, not manipulation. She thought I was interesting, and she could let me know that as a curious woman, not a come-on. This went on for some time, until we had learned just about everything we were going to learn about each other with our clothes on. And probably more than if we'd taken them off. The question that dawns on everyone at this point, however, is the same one that occurred to Harry and Sally: Can men and women ever really be friends? Was the fake orgasm good for him, too?

I've tried not to fake date since the night I was fake proposed to. No man could listen to Meg Ryan moan in the diner and go home and have a good night's sleep. Much less every weekend. But I retain a certain fondness, a self-righteousness. Dating was never supposed to be anything more than a formality, a parlor game, and now, like grim Vince Lombardi, we've made it everything. We're so obsessed with scoring, we don't stop to listen to the band in the stands or dance the Macarena in the end zone, just because we can. It's too bad. Fake dating is the only time that something fake may spur more honesty. More than once, my fake dates confessed things they never would have if we'd been heading home together. The kinds of things that would have been way too much for "lovers" to handle. Of course, this learning process is the reason for fake dating in the first place. Perhaps now I'll learn there is something to be said for not knowing, for the sweet veil of ignorance. "Taking the plunge" they call it, when a relationship leaps into motion. But after fake dating, it may seem like only swimming in the shallows.

HE SAID/SHE SAID

- "If you say you're gonna make me dinner, don't make me grilled cheese."

- "I can't believe you can't validate my inability to forgive you!"

- "Take that!" I said, throwing a picture of Buddha at her.

- "I'm emotionally unavailable."

- During the breakup he composed the sentence "Madness is my suit of size" in magnetic fridge poetry.

- "When you laugh so loud, it makes me feel alienated."

- In an attempt to explain why we were incompatible, he told me, "But you really *like* to help people."

- "Men who do improv make bad fathers."

- "You don't like 'Modern Marvels'?!?" (The History Channel TV show)

- *"Oh my God. You're fired,"* I said to him when he'd shared something with his family I didn't want him to. After his brother-in-law found out the thing shared was meant to be private, he said, "I think that, for the future, you need to draw clear lines concerning what he can and cannot share with the extended family. However, this was worth anything he may suffer."

- "The flat tax is *so* problematic."

- "Just take a look at the spreadsheet (fig. 1) I'm e-mailing you," he said. We were on the phone arguing about our long-distance relationship and who should move. He thought he was being constructive.

POSSIBILITIES FOR A&A (Fig. 1)

OPTION	YEAR	AMY	ANDREW	SAME LOCATION
1	Year 1	NYC Cleary	Geneva GF or DC FoF	
	Year 2	NYC Cleary	Boston KSG/HBS	
	Year 3	NYC LLM	Boston KSG/HBS	
	Year 4	Open	Boston KSG/HBS	Possible
2	Year 1	NYC Cleary	Boston KSG/HBS	
	Year 2	NYC Cleary	Boston KSG/HBS	
	Year 3	NYC LLM	Boston KSG/HBS	
	Year 4	Open	Open	Possible
3	Year 1	NYC Cleary	Boston KSG/HBS	
	Year 2	Boston HSPH	Boston KSG/HBS	Yes
	Year 3	NYC Cleary	Boston KSG/HBS	
	Year 4	Open	Open	Possible
4	Year 1	DC Cleary	DC FoF	Yes
	Year 2	Boston HSPH	Boston KSG/HBS	Yes
	Year 3	DC or NYC Cleary	Boston KSG/HBS	
	Year 4	Boston Clerkship	Boston KSG/HBS	Yes
5	Year 1	NYC LLM	Boston KSG/HBS	
	Year 2	Boston HSPH	Boston KSG/HBS	Yes
	Year 3	DC or NYC Cleary	Boston KSG/HBS	
	Year 4	DC or NYC Cleary	Open	Possible

THE X-FACTOR

by Sasha Cagen

It was a Sunday afternoon in November, and I was about to meet Bachelor No. 4 in my new campaign to be open-minded about the possibilities of online dating. As I biked to meet Tom at a teahouse—a chaste first date if there ever was one—I cleared my head and promised myself I would not expect immediate lust. Maybe it was just a nod toward reality; when you meet someone randomly, on the basis of a picture, a profile, and a few coy e-mails, the chances of mutual attraction are not great. Not surprisingly, the sight of Tom (5′ 7″, an inch shorter than me, clad in gray wool slacks and navy sweater) standing on the sidewalk, did not turn me on. He just wasn't my type. But over the next four hours of tea and conversation, something strange transpired.

Previous online dates had felt like job interviews, with thrilling Q&A sessions about siblings and the inevitable "How long have you lived in San Francisco?" But with Tom, I felt like I'd hit the online dating jackpot: the conversation was natural and free-flowing. When we parted there was no kiss, but we both clearly stated we'd like to see each other again. I just wanted to keep talking.

Our second date, four days later: *The Motorcycle Diaries*. My suggestion, and a mistake, I realized, as soon as the first scene began. Note to self: Never go to a movie starring Gael García Bernal with someone you are not overwhelmingly attracted to. It's just not fair to anyone involved. Tom is Yale-educated, and not in a George Bush sort of way, but he had no pretensions: He confessed that he didn't realize *The Motorcycle Diaries* was about Che Guevara until the very end. He thought the film was just an artsy movie about two guys on a road trip across South America. That he could admit this was hilariously endearing to me. After the movie we had a couple of drinks. As we bundled up in our coats, my anxiety level started to rise. On the second date, a good-night kiss might be in order. Uh-oh.

That was the problem with dating Tom. I liked him so much, an abnormal amount. He was smart, funny, thoughtful, and he did all the right things with confidence. He called me without playing games. I felt a singular calm around him, a bubble in which other worries did not intrude. But there was no heat. For whatever reason, whether some unknowable lack of pheromones between us or his demeanor (more nice than commanding), gentle kissing was all I could muster in the way of sexual interaction. Inviting him inside my house seemed almost unthinkable.

The answer to my dilemma should have been easy: Don't continue to see people you are not attracted to. But when everything else is there—an emotional connection, pitch-perfect banter, a great ease between two people—and time is marching on, friends' wedding invitations continuing to appear in the mailbox, it's increasingly hard to slam the door on the myth of gradual attraction. Especially in light of my recent parade of Internet dates, in which Generic Internet Date asks, "Where have you traveled?" and I feel like I'm in seventh grade, listing off the names of countries I have visited.

The question remained, however: How long do you wait to figure out whether there's an "X-factor"? It's one thing to become inadvertently gradually attracted to a colleague or someone in a yoga class you see every week. But it's another to schedule multiple dates, premeditatedly waiting for the touch of someone's arm to send a shiver down your spine.

Complicating the situation, I met Tom soon after my birthday. With every year, my theories about love and partnership get revised. In the past I either knew immediately—yes or no way—but becoming an adult seems to be about embracing this middle ground, playing wait and see. Now that I'm thirty-one, the notion of love at first sight (or a passionate, flirtatious discussion that lasts until four in the morning) seems immature. So many women have told me they weren't initially attracted to their husbands, that sometimes that story seems like the norm—the adult approach to love. But is it asking too much to want a cue, maybe a tiny spark of electricity within the first couple meetings?

In my mind the beginning of the relationship is supposed to be relatively effortless—a time when you can't keep your hands off each other. When you rent movies and you rarely make it to the end. But now that I am in my thirties, less married to my work and more desirous of a real boyfriend, or, dare I say, a life partner, I wonder if growing up means ditching the need for instant sexual attraction. Perhaps the X-factor would emerge over time.

Around this time, a coworker told me the story of meeting her husband through Match.com. She could take him or leave him on the first date, but by date five, they were groping each other during dinner. I decided five would be my magic number—enough time to let love bloom, but not so long that I would lead Tom on or get stuck in a lustless relationship of fake kissing. For the most part, we had fun. On date number four, we were on our way to see another movie, and I wondered out loud whether it was immoral to smuggle a bottle of Diet Coke under my jacket into a struggling neighborhood movie house. Tom laughed and said that I must feel guilty about a lot of things. Once again, Tom got me. I got him. He thought my neurotic flaws were cute. But still, when he was about to drop me off, a lump rose in my throat, a physical feeling I've felt since high school when I'm on a date with a guy I don't want to kiss. My body revolts and tells me, *Sasha, get out of the car.*

Being single is not hard for me. I like my freedom. But occasions like these—clicking with a guy in every way minus the "spark"—brings on a wash of painful self-interrogation, making me wonder if all these years of being single are because there's something *wrong* with me. Have I shriveled up inside? Have I become evil and critical? Am I afraid of intimacy, of being with a guy who likes me and is actually available? Why *can't* I be physically attracted to this exceptional person? Do I just not want to be happy? Am I afraid of my life not living up to a movie? Worst of all, is this a symptom of something even darker: a subconscious, self-destructive belief that I don't really deserve the nice guy? As someone who feels comfortable alone, and has *never* really settled, I have to start wondering whether the problem is me. Am I capable of being attracted to anyone?

I wish I could tell you I eventually became attracted to Tom—that a light switched on in my body that made me drag him upstairs to discover a surprise Lothario. Or that I gave up on sexual attraction and realized I'm happier with friend-as-partner-as-bosom-buddy. None of these things happened. Instead, I started to drive myself insane. I started to hear all these voices in my head—married friends, saying you don't want a fire in a mature relationship, anyway. You just want the embers. Then I asked them, "Don't you need the fire in the beginning in order to produce embers?" There's nothing like having a pretend debate about your so-called relationship by yourself.

The real question at the end of the day was this: Why couldn't I ignore the lump in my throat, take the leap, and invite Tom into bed? Why does the body matter? The answer is simple: Because it does.

There's a second brain in our bodies, located in the gut, with thousands of nerves entrenched in the lining of the esophagus, stomach, small intestine, and colon. I knew this intuitively during my twenties—that gut instincts and my body's reactions mattered. In my twenties, I never would have carried on with five weeks of self-flagellation trying to be attracted to someone I didn't even want to kiss. I would have moved on and maintained the optimistic belief that attraction and great conversation would eventually coincide. I don't want a diamond ring—I'm sure I'd lose it. And I'm not obsessed with being a bride. But recently I've become impatient with serendipity; I'm more willing to entertain thoughts of compromise. I've gone out with too many men I just never felt genuine interest in. My friends and I have talked ourselves to death about dating. With so much thinking about love, and so many strategies for finding it, I've lost confidence in my ability to know love when I see it. I've turned my love life into a social science experiment. How can romance take place under so much self-observation? This experiment with Tom had to end.

I'm someone who responds well to slogans, affirmations, and mantras to pep myself up. The new mantra that occurred to me around this time was the following: Growing up doesn't mean giving up. I repeated that to myself a few times after getting a voice mail from Tom and not feeling the oomph to call him back. I liked Tom to the ends of the earth, but all my joy at meeting a kindred spirit had drained away under the pressure of trying to turn him into a boyfriend.

Our last date (number five) was a Friday night, dinner after an art opening. After eating, we wandered through the streets of our neighborhood. Tom wanted to get a drink, but I asked if we could sit down on a nearby bench. I tried to be as precise as I could in my language. Nervous about how to break up with someone I had never really started dating, and truly wanting a friendship with him, I began my prepared speech.

"Tom, I want you to know how much I like you, I think you are a phenomenal person, I've enjoyed getting to know you so much, I've never gone on this many dates with someone from Nerve.com before."

"Get to the 'but,'" he said.

"But . . . I don't feel that our relationship is going in a romantic direction. I'm trying to say this carefully because I feel there is something special between us. I want to be your friend."

"I know what you're trying to say," he replied. "It's going to take a couple of hours for my ego to recover. But I know that what you're doing isn't easy."

In this moment of emotional honesty, really cutting to the chase, his eyes seemed so brown and open. He seemed like such a strong, real person. Maybe we were just thwarted by meeting online, through the artificial nature of dinners, cups of coffee, and movies. But *Stop, stop, stop,* I had to tell myself. No more endless ambivalence; I knew what I wanted.

We hugged. Tom said he would call me in a couple days. As I watched him walk away, I felt disappointed to watch his figure recede down the street. If experience proves correct, it's very hard and rare for a nascent friendship to recover from a dating misfire. I would be lying if I said that I didn't feel oddly happy, though, a certain buzz of elation that arrives when I've finally been honest with myself. Walking up the stairs to my studio apartment—alone on a Friday night at 10 p.m., keys jingling in my hands—I felt liberated, a spring in my step, an oh-my-God feeling. I wasn't in love, but the deed was done.

RELATIONSHIP RED FLAGS

- Listing Friendster.com status as "single."

- Being forced to watch her play the home version of *Dance Dance Revolution.*

- He had my birthday tattooed on the back of his head in the form of a bar code, then shaved his head so everyone could see it. Cashiers always used to pretend to scan him when we went shopping. When we broke up, he told me the tattoo signified "the day my best friend died."

- She only came over because I have air-conditioning. (It was a really hot summer.)

- He has a personalized license plate with his initials (that also just happen to spell out the name of his favorite soft drink).

- After a month of courtship, the sex ends and you become jealous of all the time he spends with his best friend.

- He leaned over and hocked a big spitball out the window. During sex. Without stopping. It was really, really, really unfortunate timing.

- He programmed his own version of Evite.com because it wouldn't allow him to invite enough people to his party.

- When you play music in the apartment, you want to die of embarrassment when he dances. (Not because he is a terrible dancer, but because he thinks he is extraordinarily cool and hip while dancing.) I cannot listen to that Modest Mouse CD anymore.

- She mentions that she still snuggles with her ex-boyfriend/roommate at night. "But don't worry," she says, "it's like we're siblings, not lovers."

- When you move in with him, his ex is still there—and still pays your new partner's portion of the rent.

- My (now ex-) husband brought a laptop on our honeymoon so he could play video games. When I think of the honeymoon, I remember the sound of the agonized moans of dying computer monsters: "Ugggg! Arghhhh!" Not exactly the kind of moans I'd hoped for. . . .

- She flirts with all the other men in the room—even at a family function.

- When someone else's little lacy panties are hanging off the bathroom doorknob.

- Even today, you are still unsure if he is gay or straight.

ALWAYS A BRIDESMAID

by Christina Amini

"Ooh, you must feel really left out," my niece Emma says, taunting me.

I pretend not to hear her and step into the shade of the patio umbrella. We're standing outside in the California sun, looking at photos taken minutes after my sister's recent engagement: There's the newly betrothed couple holding each other; my sister showing her ring to the camera; my sister midair, jumping with adrenaline. I have five sisters (no brothers), and all of them except me—Kim, Lisa, Dawn, Ariana, and now the youngest one, Elita—have received engagement parties like this one. My whole family is gathered at her fiancé's house, where Elita has spent the day with her future in-laws, preparing dozens of Indian dishes for the auspicious meeting of the families.

"You must feel *really* left out," Emma repeats, waiting for my response.

"Yup, I'm pretty left out," I finally retort, and then argue, "but Kim is divorced. Doesn't that count?"

Eleven-year-old Emma doesn't budge: "She *was* married." I know when it's time to go back for seconds.

With all the wedding energy in the air—the "oh, they're so sweet's," the discussion of letterpress invitations and wedding cakes and rehearsal dinners, which then leads to friendly musings about future children and the in-laws' grandparental involvement—I'm paralyzed by my place in it all. Being gay, my serious relationship is with a woman I love.

Just like the men my sisters have married, my girlfriend has also become part of our family. My niece knows that when she sees Auntie Chrissy, she's likely to see Elspeth, too. My girlfriend and I take Emma on adventures in the creek; we color Easter eggs with her; we play a mean game of Duck Duck Goose.

But at times like these, it's obvious our relationship is, well, not exactly understood. Like the time Emma toured our studio apartment and said, "God, it sucks you only have one bed. It really sucks you only have one bed." I laughed and repeated the line to Elspeth, shaking my head, raising my eyebrows, and pretend-grimacing, "God, it really sucks we only have one bed." I imagine Emma thinks that Auntie Chrissy will be Old Maid Chrissy. Just thinking about it, my jaw lowers and my face tightens. "I have a lover!" I want to shout. "She slow dances to the cha-cha with me! She makes my lunch in the morning! She is my one and only!" But instead, my other half feels invisible, and by extension, part of me disappears.

All this said, I'm not walking by jewelry shops pointing out rings I like and waiting for a proposal to validate my coupledom. After bridesmaiding for four sisters' and three friends' weddings, the luster of the registry and the mania of the details don't exactly make me jealous of wedding cake photos. I've watched my sisters move from falling in love, to the anxious anticipation of the proposal, to high-gear wedding planning. I, myself, have been on the pre-engagement counseling team, the post-engagement invitation-editing team, the window-washing team, the petunia-planting team, the music-selection team. I've scrubbed my parents' door hinges with a toothbrush for the reception and have chosen Louis Armstrong over Led Zeppelin for the first dance. Honestly, I'm a little exhausted by the upcoming prospect of our family's first Indian wedding.

My younger sister imagines some of the basic tenets of a traditional Indian wedding for her and her beloved: the attendance of at least four hundred guests (in India the whole village takes part in the celebration); an exchange of garlands among family members; the groom riding up to the wedding on a white horse; seven wedding rituals at the ceremony; tents, henna, marigolds. Though not Indian, my sister joyfully accepts her fiancé's traditions. "You are literally tied together with cloth during part of the ceremony," she gushes. "You begin your new life together." As part of the Amini Wedding Commission, I think that I can safely say we are all alternately awed by and in fear of the event. We imagine the grandeur and beauty of *Monsoon Wedding*; we also wonder how they will cut down the guest list.

But my mom is an old pro at weddings. In fact, our family is like a well-oiled wedding machine. We know where to buy the Dyeables. We know which caterers make the best spinach soufflés. We have a sister who makes the first toast, one who encourages the guests to start eating, and one who leads the dancing. Three of the weddings have taken place at my parents' house, so we have addressed such intimate details as bathroom traffic-flow and parking issues. In the midst of diagramming table arrangements, I, perhaps like any bridesmaid sister, stop to imagine my own relationship at the center of the excitement. Someday I want the spotlight for us, too.

My dear Elspeth and I have just celebrated our third anniversary—the first anniversary in a Brooklyn apartment, the second in a studio in Northern California, the third with graduate-school-induced long-distance care packages. My younger sister's engagement marked her four-year anniversary, but I imagine that Elspeth and I will take longer to come to that decision. The roads behind and before us are less paved, and we need to know what our commitment to each other will mean before we declare it.

Sometimes, snuggling into bed at night, we dream of our own future family. We whisper to each other, "Let's be together forever. Okay?" And we hold each other tight, as if the closer we sleep, the more we will seep into each other. Like many gay and straight couples, we're on the way there, but we're not quite there—there are ways that we need to learn to be together before we can make the big commitment.

I admit it, I am impatient. My littlest sister is getting married, and suddenly I want to be ready now, too. How old will I be when I'll want to do this? Thirty? Forty? Fifty? Which one hundred and fifty people will feel comfortable watching "the bride may now kiss the bride"? How many more bachelorette party games must I plan before it's my turn? And what does it mean to be "ready," anyway?

Elspeth recently escorted me to our first wedding together: a formal, public date—a warm-up for the Indian Fusion Wedding. When "Everybody Dance Now" came on the loudspeakers, able-bodied people hit the dance floor. Elspeth, a reserved, old-fashioned beauty convinced to wear a strapless dress, found me salsaing with my younger sister. She cut in and held me to her. I squirmed a little, then twirled myself under her arms. I led her through a series of tricky arm lifts and spins, the same way that I had with my sister. Somewhere, outside the slippery tile of the dance room, my parents talked with family friends.

Elspeth resisted my dynamic moves and pulled me tighter. As I salsaed my hips away from hers, I whispered in her ear, "The bride's granny does *not* need to see this." "She'll see it sometime," Elspeth responded and held me beneath my shoulder blades. "And what does she care, anyway?" She pressed the polka dots of her party dress to the sky blue ribbing of mine.

Between our fourth and fifth glasses of champagne, the bride announced the toss of her bridal bouquet. "Anybody unmarried, get out here. Girls. Boys. Come on up!" The bride turned her back and lofted her white freesias high into the afternoon. With the intensity of a rebounding basketball player, Elspeth grabbed the bouquet and pulled it down. Giggling at herself, she delightedly rushed me for a hug. The photographer took our picture.

On good days I've imagined our wedding into a big party. I invite all of our friends, we eat good food, and we dance to bad eighties music. However, most days, marriage and anxiety tie the knot, and the whole idea of my commitment becomes a personal test. Potentially anxiety-inducing details materialize: I predict my great-aunt's confusion by the invitation, my mom explaining the ceremony to her friends, and the constant comparison to the other weddings. Then my own homophobia percolates through my stomach: Am I worth the stage? Am I worth celebrating?

Weddings, and the concomitant showers and bachelorette parties, are a rite of passage, especially in my family. I keep wondering how it might happen for me. Can I get the father-daughter dance? The wedding photo on the piano? Who will propose? Will we register? Who will pay? And then I'm suddenly suffocating in the wedding frenzy I detest.

"Chris-*tee*-na," Emma whines, snapping me back to the reality of the buffet table. "Come *on*! Will you come with me to get some dessert?"

When we return to the patio outside, the embarrassed young couple is reluctantly reenacting the proposal per the in-laws' request. The groom's parents sing a playful Hindi song about the groom's future subservience. My father raises a glass, saying, "I understand that, in both of our traditions, marriage is about bringing two families together." The families clink glasses.

It is then I realize a wedding's function: to help a couple embark on a new phase of life with the support of its loved ones. And I realize this is what I want for Elspeth and me: for the whole community to support us in our love, the whole town to show up and cheer, for my mom to want to dance. The scale of the Indian wedding lets the new couple know the magnitude of this commitment. I want my love to be big, serious, festive.

My niece pulls up a chair. I'm still a little bit defensive after the "You must feel *really* left out" comment. She scoots closer to me.

"So, Christina, who are you dating?"

I pause, nibble my samosa, swallow, then say, "Elspeth."

This is the first time she or I have been so bold. I sip my wine. She sips her apple cider. Will she fumble? Will I? How will she react to the news?

"I thought so." My niece notes my expression. "But I was right, you aren't *engaged*," she says.

Not yet, I think. *Not yet.*

Editors' note: Just before this book went to press, Christina and Elspeth got engaged.

TOP TEN SIGNS HE MIGHT NOT BE PRINCE CHARMING

by Opal Desaire

Aaaahh, the monumental first vacation with a new boyfriend—though he was not exactly new. In fact, he was a recycled college boyfriend who had been melted down and transformed into a mostly functioning adult. Nevertheless, we had been reunited by a mutual friend and were happily paired for five months. Because it was January in Minnesota, the inevitable "vacation talk" began. My twenty-six-year-old boyfriend was adamant about going to Orlando to see Mickey. I was pretty open to going anywhere as long as it was cheap, and Florida seemed warm and relaxing.

1. Five straight "magical days," not so many magical nights.
2. Matching outfits. (I didn't notice until the fourth day, but each morning he waited until I was dressed to select his matching outfit—a practice I'd always attributed to the fifty-five-and-over set.)
3. All Disney channels, all the time. (Our hotel on the Disney premises did not support regular cable, just cartoons and the Disney propaganda channel.)
4. Two cases of Slim-Fast. (His. How is it that I ended up paying for it?)

5. Willing to stand in line for forty minutes to watch mechanical dolls, but complained nonstop about the line at the airport.

6. Five hundred Christmas cards to sign and address, two weeks late. (He was supposed to have sent all of his customers a holiday card. I was recruited for labeling and stuffing on the plane ride.)

7. Annoyed with "all the kids" at the Magic Kingdom.

8. Highlight of his day: seeing Lilo.

9. Getting drunk at Epcot. (We had a few too many margaritas in Mexico.)

10. Red, four-inch high-heeled sandals (his Christmas gift to me on the trip and part of his deep-rooted Jessica Rabbit fetish).

ON FINDING THE IT GUY: AN INQUIRY INTO THE YOU'LL KNOW THEORY

by Shoshana Berger

I always imagined he would be blond. Blond and rangy and slightly hunched like an Olympic swimmer. His skin would have a sunny chlorine smell, which I would love so much, I'd nuzzle my head against the nape of his neck and just inhale deeply instead of kissing him. Something about that scent meant he'd always be better than me. Faster. More pure. As I grew older, I learned that women tend to prefer dark men—Clark Kent stand-ins, with meaty shoulders and chin scruff by lunch. To me there was something sweaty and primitive about that kind of man. Mostly, they made me think about hair, and the great bushels of it there would be once he removed his shirt and pants. I pictured Leonardo's Vitruvian Man, legs and arms akimbo, but with the lineaments obscured by a thick wooly pelt. No doubt he'd shed during our (vigorous) lovemaking, and while he put his jeans back on, I'd lie there naked, crooking my neck to gaze down at my breasts and belly and remove, one by one, all the squiggly black lines. This plucking ritual would surely insult anyone who paid attention, but I would fear that if I left them there, the hairs might actually graft into my skin.

Still, I gave all the men a chance. Everyone deserves a chance! It wasn't hard to give up on finding chlorine boy when the others were funny, or had great apartments, or possessed some preternatural sense of how to break me down. A few case studies: No. 1 would come over on Friday nights to cook a five-course meal for my mother and sister and me. The dinners involved a lot of sautéing, and reduction, and often went on past midnight. He was bossy, and very skilled in the kitchen. After a few drinks at parties, No. 2 would pull the bottom of his T-shirt up and through the neck like teenage girls do, then dance around like a drunk uncle at a wedding, slapping his midriff. He foamed over with self-love, and really knew how to light up a room. No. 3 used such obscure, Churchillian language, I had to write things down during our phone conversations and look them up afterward. He was chronically depressed but had a great way with words.

I learned important things from Nos. 1, 2, and 3, like how to remove the smell of garlic from my fingers, how to stand up on my bike and lean into a hill, and how, after sex, to run my fingers over a man's back lightly, like the tingly fadeout of a song. Life lessons, and I am glad I know them. Still, it was clear within minutes of meeting all of those guys what would end it. After talking for a while, a sad smile would form behind my lips. The smile said, *Now you know how this will end.* And no matter how hard I tried to wipe that knowledge away, when the time came to break up, I'd nod, with tight lips, and say, *I knew how this would end,* with great sanctimony, like a nihilist being asked for comment after Armageddon. But the world hasn't ended, and with luck, won't in the sixty-odd years I have left, anyway. So I kept gambling, folding the numbered men, hoping that one fine day fate would deal me a royal flush. After a long stint of betting and folding, I started to wonder: Was I just unlucky? Would I ever find my It Guy?

How to increase your odds of finding the It Guy (IG): Get invited to as many weddings as you can. Weddings have the highest incidence of IGs. The reasons for this are clear:

1. There are a limited number of single people, and it will be obvious who they are *(Me me me, pick me!)*
2. Having been invited, you and prospective IGs already have at least one mutual friend.
3. Everyone will be drunk.
4. The stage is set for you by the newlyweds, who have gathered you all to bear witness to the eternal sunshine of their love.

The end of the numbered men: I took someone I'd been seeing for a few months—amiable guy, a few years older than me, Irish—to a wedding. I'm drawn to the Irish for their insane writers and aptitude for holding their liquor. So much so that after college I convinced my father and sister to accompany me on a self-conceived William Butler Yeats tour. We drove through muggy bogs, and past peat farmers, thatched roofs, and fields of the greenest green you've ever seen to pay homage to all of the sites in Yeats's poems: Ben Bulben, Innisfree, Sligo. Wanting to fit in, I made sure to pick up an accent. I asked locals for directions in my best brogue: "Can you tell us, please, where we might find Crazy Jane's Pub? You're too kind." My sister began to walk several paces behind me.

But back to the wedding with the Irishman. He was really only of Irish descent, which was a few generations back (but I know a lineage when I see one). He was a woodworker and had tanned hands with long, bony fingers that looked good in silver rings. Like all woodworkers, he acted slightly superior and tried aggressively to make people laugh. I hate jokes, but he was exceedingly good at telling them, and he would look at me tenderly after finishing one, as if to say, *Thank you for laughing. I know you're reaching beyond yourself.*

I was late to pick him up, and didn't like the way he was dressed. As we argued on the way there, I concentrated all of my superpowers on ejecting him from the passenger seat (with a parachute, of course; I'm not a violent person). I kept thinking, *I don't accept this person at all. Not at all.* But then, you don't want to hurt anyone, and even if having him at the wedding detracts from pursuing IG, you need someone to put his arm around you while your friends go off into Happyland, lest an arctic wind of loneliness knock you down, leaving you to die a horrible, hypothermic death right there in front of all of their (married) friends. So you hold out.

During the post-vow champagne toast, which took place in a rustic old army bunker with lead-paned windows and wooden floors, I was catching up with a girlfriend (married), when I spotted a potential IG across the room. I'd known him casually for a couple of years, but we'd never exchanged more than a few words—I'd once asked him to be a model for the magazine I edit (he politely declined), and we had a brief flirtation at a party, which was hastily interrupted by the older sister of a girlfriend with whom he'd just broken things off. His shaggy, coal-black hair kept flopping in front of his eyes, then getting pushed back with a flick of the head—a little dance routine he did every few minutes. He was wearing a dark gray suit and an electric blue tie.

"Is that _____?" I asked my girlfriend, who also knew him.

"I think it is," she said, craning her neck to get a look at his face. "He set these two up. So today is a good omen for him."

"He looks different with long hair," I said, trying to sound casual. I couldn't take my eyes off of him.

At a break in the conversation, I made my way over. The Irishman sidled up and said something typical about wanting to get me drunk so we could make up properly. I kept walking right up to IG.

"Hi?" I said, calling him by his name.

"Hi, I thought I saw you over there," he said, eyes flashing. It went on from there, with all the usual what-have-you-been-up-to questions. After a few minutes of watching us talk, the Irishman got the point and made off for the bar.

"Can I get you two anything?" he asked, sneering. *(Yes, get lost!)*

In that first interchange with IG, I thought he was flattering, nervous, and maybe a little dense. I made some cracks and got blank stares in return. I began to fear that IG was just a beautiful airhead. When I returned to the Irishman, who was talking to my girlfriend and her husband, he insisted that we play who-would-you-sleep-with-at-this-wedding? I'd never heard of the game, but apparently it exists.

"Everyone does this at weddings!" the Irishman cried.

I scanned the room unconvincingly.

"Let me guess," he said, "the guy from Oasis?" He looked IG's way.

"Puhleeze," I said, rolling my eyes. "That guy has no sense of humor."

Question: How do you know they're just a lead-in and not IG? It's a perplexing problem, and I know of no satisfying answer. You have no idea what IG is like until you meet him, so you apply a glossy varnish to the one you're with *(So loyal! He'll be a great dad!)*. There is much of the fairy tale in this, with all the bad princessy aftertaste you might expect. But no matter how good you are at masking the truth, there are no understudies for IG and no one suddenly transforms into him. Doubts about your latest prince grow dark and fragrant, like water seeping into soil. And once that doubt has taken root, there's no stopping it from greening. All the ways in which you don't agree on music and books begin to pollinate and unfurl like giant blooms of wrongness. This all leads up to an emotionally gruesome moment, when you're sitting in a car together late at night, after a party where things went badly. You look at him in the half-light and his face begins to peel back, and you realize he is not your prince at all; you've been terribly mistaken. Do not feel bad, as though you should have known all along. We all want to believe.

We say: *I'm the one with the problem. I should accept him exactly as he is, made in God's own image.* Or, conversely: *This man is no good. Why am I always choosing bad men?*

I tell the Irishman, tearfully and with real regret, that although his hands are among the most beautiful I've ever seen, I just can't continue. He wants to know why and I tell him, "It's just me, I'm searching for the impossible." He says, "No, I know there are specific reasons. Don't worry, I can take it." And I say, "No no no, it's me, it's me." But he keeps pressing until I finally blurt out all of the obvious reasons why he's not IG and never will be. His face falls like a deflated balloon. Lesson learned: Never tell people the real reasons why you are breaking up with them.

As I drove home from his house, I considered my situation. I'm thirty-five. I have approximately five years left to procreate safely. I haven't been in love for close to a decade. And, when exposed in direct sunlight, I see that my feelings for my first chlorine boy were driven by his total immersion in everything except me. That had me hooked for a while. But once I got him to fall for me, the winds shifted and a yellow mist of ambivalence moved in, rubbed its muzzle on the windowpanes, and swallowed me in a toothless fog. From then on, that was the pattern: Fight hard to win them over, then duck.

I guess I'll just live alone, like Emily Dickinson or a Brontë sister. I'll write veiled poems about sex and death from a musty turret in which I've shut myself. (You can live in those, right? I'd build a platform to sleep on. Stand on milk crates to reach the tiny window at the top.) Or I'll join a book club and meet other Still-Single Women who enjoy Irish literature and are always free to meet on Friday nights. Or I'll get a dog and meet dog people at the dog park. Maybe a few of us SSWs could get a house together up north and start birding, or studying mushrooms. What's that called again? Not fungology—something more scientific-sounding.

I could find ways to be happy. So what if it wasn't the booming, THX sort of happiness—the feeling of sea spray on your cheeks while kissing at the bow of the ship, or slow dancing to a jukebox as the owlish bartender looks on and smiles, or the lens flare off goggles as you flee the scene in a prop plane, red scarves flapping in the wind. Instead, it would be the happiness equivalent of an after-dinner mint, left on a pillow, in an airport hotel room.

My newly married friend comes back from her honeymoon, and I e-mail her the next day:

Subject: That was fun!
From: <sb>
So what's up with IG? Is he seeing anyone?

Subject: Re: That was fun!
From: <ah>
Isn't he brilliant and gorgeous and perfect? Unfortunately, he's not over his ex, and he's so indecisive it'll drive you crazy. Trust me on this one.

Pause. Eat. Sleep. Before bed do a St. Agnes's Eve ritual: Concentrate very hard on IG, in hopes that dreams will reveal something I can grasp hold of. A sign.

Next day:

Subject: Re: Re: That was fun!
From: <ah>
Forget everything I said! I just heard that IG's been asking about you nonstop since our wedding! Call him!!!

I'm no fool. Why would I wipe all of her incrimination from the record just because he showed the faintest sign of interest? No doubt he's rebounding (or worse, he can't decide whether he's over her or not!). He's the kind of guy who spells M-u-t-u-a-l A-s-s-u-r-e-d D-e-s-t-r-u-c-t-i-o-n.

So I e-mail him.

After a month together we say the L word. My breath gets short when I talk about him with friends. He comes to a family Thanksgiving and my mother yells from the head of the table that he must be pawing me because I have a scratch on my arm. I've had glimmers of this feeling over the years, but it hasn't hung around since I first fell for a boy with chlorine skin when I was eighteen years old.

It's December and IG's birthday. We've been together for two months. I take him for the weekend to a sort of upscale hunter's lodge where there's a taxidermied buck or bobcat on every wall. After dinner we go to our bearskin-rug room and light a fire in the fireplace (he stacks the logs perfectly, with pockets of air, like a scout). I give him his gifts: a few CDs of all the songs we like, and a tie with a horse on it, and a little piece of a map with a message on it that I've rolled up inside a plastic capsule. He opens it all very quickly, then suddenly deflates, sinking into the couch with a sigh so voluminous, it holds everything he's ever wished for, or lost.

"I don't know what to do with you," he says.

"Let's just buck convention," I say boldly. "Let's go fast." He knows exactly what that means. It means we should get married. And soon.

People will have many theories about how *you know* you've found IG, but they are all equally bootless. Those who are lucky enough to be married or in love will tell you "Oh, You'll Know." This will seem like a heap of shit. Oh really? *How* will I know? Will I have a hot flash? Suddenly break out into song? So many well-intentioned people gave me that answer. "But aren't there exceptions?" I'd ask. "Couldn't I be a defective model without the proper sensor?" But it turns out that all along, the *You'll Know* people were right. I agree—it's terribly annoying for me to be saying this now that I've found mine, but it happens to be true. Only the most undeserving of people—those who were dictators or meter maids or jellyfish in a former life—are excluded from the eventuality of finding one. And when he finally does arrive *(You might have come a little sooner!)*, you'll know, after a very short time (maybe even on that first night!), that he's the real deal. Suddenly everything that came before will burn up in a great medieval pyre. The sky will part, bells will clang, and peasant girls will dance barefoot in the streets. Your search is over!

Three months later, at a fancy hotel he's booked for the weekend, IG takes me out on a high promenade with a view of the ocean. Under a moon that looks like a hole in the sky that someone's shining a light through, he gets down on bended knee and proposes. It's a scene that I'd rewound and played back endlessly since I was a teenager. The way I imagined it, I'd suddenly become the happiest creature alive, happier than monkeys swinging from branches, or beavers finishing their dams. But in the end it's just two people, still a little awkward around each other, and maybe a little drunk, pretending that they know how to act during a proposal.

All very nice, you say, but how does this confirm or disprove the
You'll Know **theory?** What I'm trying to say—it's a bitter pill for the unconverted, I realize—is that it really is a matter of holding out. Of waiting for something who's so good, forces beyond your comprehension move things from the I'll Never Do This pile to the I'll Do Anything With You pile, which gets so big, it begins to block everyone else out of the picture.

After so many years as a nonbeliever, I've now become an apostle of the *You'll Know* theory. How do *I know* that I've found IG? Because he's someone who no mate-matching database or astrological chart could predict: He talks to himself, leaves little notes in my books that I find later, and has the exact opposite body type from me, so that we could put our two halves together and be a perfect being. Because he used the word "lacuna" on our first date, cries when he leaves me at the airport, speaks to me on the phone in a formal, all-business manner when there are people in his office, and doesn't break even when I make googly noises. Because he likes it when I read him to sleep, is funnier than me but too shy to show off, can't pack for a trip without having a meltdown, and looks just like the blue-eyed horseman who gallops me out of the woods as violins play. Because in the middle of the night he rises from the fishy fathoms of sleep long enough to say "I Love You," then rolls over and dives back down again.

These and other things have proved to me the unassailability of the *You'll Know* theory. I'm not saying that everything will be easy once you find him. We Homo sapiens are too complicated for that to be the case. But as a famous person once said, things that give off light must endure burning. Wait for that bright light. I couldn't have written those words before. I just *didn't know*. But then I did, just as you will. Trust me on this one.

UNACCEPTABLE DATING BEHAVIOR

- Went out with a compulsive liar who claimed to have become a millionaire by inventing the pumpkin carving kit (but who later said she didn't have a cell phone because they cost so much money).

- Date's car progressively fell apart; second half of date spent holding back door closed with rope found in trunk.

- Admitting she'd LexisNexised me before our blind date.

- On our first date, he squeezed himself into the chair with me rather than sitting "all the way across the table" in his own chair.

- Date insisted on driving enormous yellow Nissan Xterra two blocks to coffee shop rather than walking ("I'm from L.A.").

- After our first date (which didn't go well), he called my mom and asked her to tell me to return his calls.

- He gargles with vodka in the morning.

- Upon meeting me in a coffee shop, he said, "I'd like to get to know you better. Want to go help me buy underwear?"

- He showed up wearing a denim jacket with Winnie the Pooh characters embroidered on it. He was thirty-five years old.

- He bought gifts for his girlfriends in bulk, had them wrapped at the department store, and kept them under the seat of his pickup. He gave me a ride home right after Christmas and handed me a bottle of eighty-dollar perfume. Clearly, he had overstocked. (I sold the perfume on eBay.)

- Rebound Boy. He licked my face. He. Licked. My. Face.

- He has a hot tub in his building and keeps a wardrobe of women's swimsuits on hand, one in every size.

- He was a sculptor who collected roadkill animals so he could use their bones in his art. He admitted that he had been "tempted" to pick up a skunk he saw while we were driving together, but he opted not to because I was a vegetarian.

FROM COSTCO TO

YOGA AND BACK

PEAKING AT TEN

by Anna Chlumsky

I am applauded every day. Not in the traditional sense—no thunderous claps, bravas, or standing ovations to seven curtain calls after a luminous rendition of Ibsen or Brecht. (Not yet, anyway.) No, I am praised on the subway, at the corner deli, at my regular bistro from the table next to me, at Starbucks as my barista hands me my tall vanilla latte. And the kudos sound like this: "I know you from somewhere. . . ." "Aren't you that girl?" "Wait, you're My Girl, aren't you?" "You have no idea how much that movie meant to me." "You made me cry."

When I was little—heck, even up to a year ago—this type of attention was a downright daily struggle. I knew they meant well, but these folks embarrassed me in front of my junior high companions and my college friends. They singled me out when all I wanted was to forget that I used to be "special." It wasn't a pleasant sort of admiration either; they reminded me of the rejections of my adolescence. I dreaded explaining my waning appearances on screen. *Why haven't they seen me work in so long?* I wanted it all to go away with the snap of a finger.

All through high school, at the height of my insecurities, the lure of Hollywood was my only ambition. I practiced my Oscar acceptance speech and my *Vanity Fair* poses in the mirror. I spent all my time memorizing screenplay sides and driving to auditions. Acting had been my life since I was ten months old, and I knew no other system. Wake up, go to school, explain to your buddies that you don't have a limousine, pretend to eat lunch by downing a can of pop, go home, fix your face, and drive to the agency. All to a chorus of "You're too fat" and "You're too young."

I longed for the days when I had the birds and the bees explained to me by the lovely Jamie Lee Curtis. The days when Jean-Claude Van Damme cut in front of me while I waited in the Porta Potti line at the *Last Action Hero* premiere. The Fourth of July I spent in Rob Reiner's pool with Elijah Wood, or the time I played with Paula Abdul's pug at the beach. The night I "ummed" my way through thanking my dog and teachers for the Best Kiss award on MTV. (Not to mention getting kissed on the forehead by Luke Perry!)

I had been given a glimpse of what VH1 tells you "making it" is. But in order to realize what *my* version of "making it" would be, I'd need to purge theirs. By the end of high school it had grown painful to want something so badly and seem to get so little in return for my efforts. I could barely look myself in the zit-magnifying mirror, let alone tackle an entire industry that thought I wasn't good enough.

When the *Entertainment Tonight* folks interviewed me as a blond, ponytailed preteen, sitting in a monogrammed director's chair, they asked me what I wanted to be when I grew up. "A horse dentist." "A paleontologist." "A journalist," I said. Even though the footlights had always been my dream, it was never the answer for my *real* life. It was what I did for fun. My *dream* life. A more serious study would surely put me on a path to success.

So, when the time came, I chose to study international relations, assuming my entire adolescent life had been enough drama. I limited my stage appearances to our university's black box theater; I thought college would end the years of low self-esteem and self-loathing. And for four years it did. I breathed easy behind the sheltered walls of Higher Learning, sporting my maroon University of Chicago sweatshirt with the words WHERE FUN COMES TO DIE emblazoned on the back. I relished burying my nerdy little head in the musty library volumes on guerilla war tactics, Aztec sacrifice, and the Tokugawa shogunate. I built my brain, my confidence, and what I thought was a life far away from the dreamworld of showbiz. In academia, if I worked hard enough, I could make a paper better, or I could get a better grade. With acting, success seemed out of my control. After years of repeated rejections, it was getting hard not to take things personally. Even if I did my best, I *still* might not be a "fit" for the role. I wasn't really sure if I still had "what it takes" to get to the top.

As soon as I graduated, I moved to New York. Don't ask why. I robotically used to say it was because of a fact-checking job for a restaurant guide, but I could have found that in any city. In truth, it seemed like an invisible hand was pushing me to this place where people come to "make it." I wanted to make it just like everyone else, but I wasn't sure what I'd make it as. I tried my hand as a freelance food and travel writer, but I found myself, ironically, much hungrier than I'd hoped. I then tapped into my not-so-inner geek and set my sights on editing science fiction and fantasy—by far the most fun nine-to-five I can imagine. (I handled dragons and spaceships daily, and the salary was better than freelance.) Although the cramped cubicles and fluorescent light felt like a foreign habitat to someone who thrived under the bright lights of the stage, the office was easier to accept than to admit I had denounced my childhood ambitions.

But, even in the grand abyss of New York City, where people get lost so easily, the subway fans haunted me. "I remember your eyes."

"You were so good." "Good luck to you." "You can go far." Finally, the familiar question, "Why aren't you acting anymore?" demanded my honest answer.

I had been crying on my lunch break from my office job. Crying was something I did often. Oh, I cried. I'd cry for no reason. I'd cry to my parents, my friends over things like "I just feel so confused" or "I just need to make it all fit together." What? Those weren't even concrete thoughts! Emotional drivel, for pity's sake! They came from some limbo place where twentysomethings dwell. A place where we want to act like grown-ups, but we still want someone else to provide us with the answers.

I was sniveling quietly past my deli, when a run-of-the-mill psychic stopped me on the street saying she "had a message" for me. You know, one of those psychics who say they see the name beginning with a *J* in your life because that's the most common letter for male names? I rolled my eyes and walked toward my office, pretending that was really where I wanted to be for the last ten minutes of my lunch break. But she persisted. She left her post and followed me a whole block, trying to get her "message" across. She caught my shoulder, and I whipped around to hear her out. She said, "You were in *My Girl*, weren't you?" Wow. Good psychic. She deserved her fifty dollars per half hour for such good intuition. Then she said, "You're not happy." Don't strike a nerve, lady, I'm fragile today. "You still want to be in show business." Crap. Crap. Crap. Don't make me confront what I've suppressed for the past six years. Please, don't! "You're not finished with it. You still have more to go."

Who am I? And who am I going to be? Was I destined to be like my father, who tells martini-laden stories about playing his tenor sax on 1960s Rush Street, though it's been years since he's whetted a reed? Or like my Uncle Vince, whose friends still refer to him as "the quarterback," even though he roughed up his knee thirty years ago? Maybe succeeding at this lifelong dream of mine was not in fact as daunting as Tara Lipinski trying to match a gold medal after the age of fourteen. Could I actually *do* it? Should I actually *try*?

I paid the lady ten bucks for ten minutes. I know, I know . . . waste of money. But I needed to do it—I had a desperate desire for answers. The psychic didn't tell me anything I didn't know already, but after I left her lair of dangling beads and colored crystals, I went home and dragged out my 8 x 10 photo of the Three Stooges, signed personally to their old vaudevillian pal my Great Grandpa Jim, who wrestled a bear before a captivated crowd in the days of the Palace and Orpheum Circuit. There was *his* legacy, the legacy of all the vaudevillians who built Broadway with their bare hands.

Suddenly what I wanted became clearer in the bright white light. I took inventory of the signs: the people on the subway, the feeling of stepping onto a stage, the little tap-dancing self in the back of my brain who kept saying, "Wait, *you* want to be in *Chicago*." I had to jump. I had to take the risk. It was time to quit the salaried job and act full-time: to dedicate my present life to the pursuit of the Great White Way and, in the meantime, play basement theaters for the love of it. It seemed I'd made my first grown-up decision by staying true to who I was as a child.

Success at a young age not only gives you a taste of grandeur and attention that you forever strive to duplicate, but it also gives you that precious sense that you can achieve absolutely anything. The trick is to learn how to let the past drive you to your next, bigger, and *better* peak. I know it will be a harder road than ever before. It'll be something more akin to the vigorous path trod by the vaudevillians than to the lucky break I got at age ten.

So perhaps my childhood success was not my peak after all. My tireless roots are burrowing much deeper—now that I've *chosen* to nurture my ambitions. I'm auditioning practically five times a day; I'm rehearsing for two openings this month; an audience just paid ten dollars apiece to see me and my friends writhe on a wet, dirty stage in the name of experimental theater. I wake up every morning eager to climb to the next peak, to the next show. And I wouldn't have it any other way.

COSTCO-OBSESSIVE DISORDER

by Carson Brown

It was Mother's Day. My brother Adam and I were both out of college, living on our own, and the empty nest feeling was hitting Mom harder than ever. When I joked about how much she wanted us back in the house, she retorted, "I want you back in the womb."

Mom loved being a mom. She especially loved to feed us. The years between 1992 and 1997 were some of the happiest of her life, as we underwent the Great Adolescent Growth Spurt. We ate almost constantly, like hummingbirds, and grew almost visibly, like plants. The marks on the doorjamb recording our heights leaped through the five-foot-somethings into the six-foot-somethings, to our basketball coaches' glee. If I skipped a crucial granola bar, my blood sugar levels plummeted until I cried about nothing and begged for intravenous orange juice. Adam was known to scramble a dozen eggs and toast a whole loaf of bread in the oven. He packed a cooler for school and drank two-thousand-calorie protein shakes for snacks. We would wolf down an extra-large pizza or split a box of Cheerios into two mixing bowls. A gallon of milk didn't last a day; our elongating bones craved it. We had left normal-portion sizes behind. To us, "family pack" meant "single serving."

Luckily for the woman responsible for our nourishment, Costco had analogously blown the top off of typical quantities. Every week Mom took the two backseats out of the minivan and loaded it with frozen waffles by the gross, eighteen-packs of pasta sauce, and cubic yards of sharp cheddar. We piled the industrial-size freezer in the garage with won tons, crab cakes, turkey burgers, chicken sticks, Hot Pockets, taquitos, and burritos. The more we ate, the better Mom felt. She had Costco to thank for facilitating this spectacular show of love.

At some point Costco replaced the regular grocery store permanently. I opened the refrigerator on Mother's Day and wondered why it was still packed with a cow's worth of ground beef. The third bay of the garage, where my first car used to sit, was now filled entirely with provisions. I couldn't walk into the walk-in pantry because it was stacked with muffin mix and pudding cups. The freezer still hummed the low hum of five-gallon mint chip drums and icy blocks of pork chops. I opened desk drawers to find that rolls of film had been multiplying like bacteria in a medium of inky pens. The house looked equipped to host the Australian national swim team, not to sustain two sedentary adults.

I tried to attribute Mom's bulk obsession to eccentricity or a fear of famine, but deep down, I worried. She could probably live on the food in her house for a year. Was this an early sign of Alzheimer's? Or a cry for help?

Shortly after the neighbors complained about the pallets of paper towel boxes blocking entry into *their* garage, Mom's ailment was diagnosed as Costco-Obsessive Disorder (COD), a disease spreading at the speed of strip malls. I share my story to give a face to this insidious affliction. By identifying the following symptoms, I hope to increase COD awareness and empower readers to combat its grip on the minds of a generation.

Symptom 1:

Increasing Inability to Discuss Anything Other Than Costco

Someone suffering from COD can relate almost any conversation to Costco. Planning a surf trip to Costa Rica? They've just started carrying wet suits. Mention Chechnyan rebels and risk hearing the story about how Gorbachev wept when he visited Costco in 1990. Those suffering from Costco-Obsessive Disorder see the store as a living part of their daily existence, a worthy topic of general interest, rather than the inconsequential errand destination it is.

Symptom 2:

An Adamant Belief That Shopping at Costco Saves Huge Sums of Money

This can be one of the most deep-seated and stubborn traits of the Costco addict. Often, a logical financial breakdown will do nothing to counter this illogical belief. The addict is paying for something beyond the product itself: the comfort of quantity.

To the detached observer, it is obvious that bulk shoppers squander more than they save. Someone afflicted by COD buys twelve tubes of toothpaste because it seems cheap, only to grow sick of the taste, throw eight of the tubes under the sink, and run out to buy another twelve-pack. It is more expensive to allow a crate of avocados to rot while intending to make guacamole rather than to forsake just three. Or what about the person who goes through five Snapples in an afternoon because there are 256 in the garage? Bought by the six-pack—or, let alone, individually—each Snapple is savored. But appetite increases with quantity at hand. When a jug of red licorice meant for a candy store is available to a nuclear family, people will eat a lot of fucking licorice.

COD sufferers need to be shown that buying something because it is perceived to be inexpensive is decidedly different from saving money. I have seen an otherwise very rational woman come home with a Costco key lime pie, beaming that it was "only eight dollars," when she already had two-thirds of an apple pie (from Costco) in her fridge. She did not need pie. She bought pie. Yet she regards Costco as a magical windfall.

Symptom 3:

Feeling the Love of Membership

Costco calls itself a "membership warehouse club" and charges forty-five dollars per year in dues. (You gotta pay to save.) At many companies, a Costco membership is considered a perk on par with profit sharing or vision care. COD, like a cult, preys on humanity's love of belonging to something exclusive. Back in the early days, Costco only sold to businesses, but later opened its doors to a "select audience of nonbusiness members" who received the privilege of access to special prices. Those with COD feel chosen, something the traditional bird-watching or bridge club can't offer.

My mom gave me a Costco card as a gift the day I left home for college. Though I shared a tiny dorm room and ate three meals a day in a cafeteria, she wanted me to feel that reassuring sense of community as I ventured out on my own. If a loved one derives self-worth from membership in any way, seek help.

Symptom 4:

Costco as Social Life

Costco's popularity has reached the point where a critical mass of the suburban population is shopping there at any given time. Comments such as "I saw Carlee Duncan's mother in line at Costco today" have become frighteningly common. The Empty Nest Set congregates at Costco. They wander the cavernous aisles, bump into one another, and exchange information about their absent children. They embrace. They sample a sausage. Costco is the town square of suburbia, its checkouts the modern sidewalk. However, responsible family members will encourage those predisposed to COD to meet friends and establish relationships outside of the Costco clubhouse.

Recently I chaperoned my mom to Costco in order to moderate her consumption. Instead, deep in COD territory, I found myself drawn to the salon-size shampoos almost unconsciously. Twenty portabello mushrooms layered under plastic wrap had a mysterious gravity of their own. Within moments I caught myself mentally calculating the cost per ounce of contact lens solution and margarita mix.

We took our place in one of the long lines, and the beep-beep-beeping of bar codes being scanned penetrated deep into my psyche. In a trance, I looked down at the flatbed cart I could barely push. An image of Mom buried under an avalanche of Costco products flashed through my mind. With superhuman strength I shoved the cart away, threw her over my shoulder, and ran for the exit. A very large quantity of our future health and happiness depended on it.

FORTY-THREE TICKETS FOR BROOKLYN

by Jordan Harrison

I'm the sort of person who can navigate a city for days without saying anything to anyone but "Medium dark roast, please." The sort of person who celebrates the advent of self check-in and the extinction of everyday pleasantries. If I feel myself turning into a regular at the restaurant on my block, I'll stay away for months. So, moving to New York two summers ago, an aspiring playwright right out of college, I thought I'd found a home where I could maintain my anonymity. But like most contact-a-phobes, I secretly hope to come across people who will disrupt my finely engineered solitude.

For much of the summer I've been telling friends about the starry cast of Anton Chekhov's *The Seagull* like P. T. Barnum announcing a parade of pachyderms: Christopher Walken, Kevin Kline, Philip Seymour Hoffman, Meryl Freakin' Streep! Not only that, the Public Theater's Shakespeare in the Park production is a freebie. Dispensed every afternoon at one o'clock, the coveted tickets are scarcer than Wonka's. Somehow my nontheater friends are blasé in the face of all this: No one is willing to set his alarm for four in the morning and join me in my quest.

5:30 a.m., Astor Place

There are no chatterboxes in the bleary-eyed line outside the Public Theater, no morning persons. Three girls with sleeping bags and designer headphones walk up, stretch out on the urine-stained sidewalk, and fall asleep again. I feel suddenly unprepared next to this slumber party, armed with nothing but a half-empty Nalgene bottle and yesterday's crossword.

These are the dog days of August, and people have started to do dramatic recitations of the heat index: "One hundred and twelve degrees! That's like the surface of Mercury!" Around 6:30 a.m., the first golden rays hit the pavement in Astor Place and bounce back a hundred times stronger into our eyes. "It begins," a woman says in a doomsday monotone, several spots behind me. It will turn out to be the hottest day of the summer. Frying-eggs-on-the-sidewalk hot. Loiter-in-the-frozen-food-aisle hot. Or, as my Texan friend likes to say, "butt-crack-sweat hot."

All is civil, if sultry, until a woman in a Public Theater T-shirt arrives at quarter to eight. She informs us that the gentleman in the blue hat waaaay up there will be the last to receive a ticket. "So there's kind of no point in you being here?" She puts a question at the end of the sentence, twisting the knife in farther. How early did Mr. Bluehat have to get here? "I saw him in line about twelve-thirty last night," she says. The increasingly power-mad woman tells us—it's already starting to feel like an "us"—that a limited number of tickets will also be dispensed today at the Pratt Institute in Brooklyn. So much for "us": I power toward the subway, leaving the blurry sleeping-bag girls in my dust.

8:30 a.m., The Pratt Institute

The sweet relief of Brooklyn: a patch of green in place of a parking lot, sprinklers gently misting the air, an attractive couple reading *The*

Seagull out loud to pass the time. A woman in a gray shift dress, a pale
artist named Marsha, sits one spot ahead of me. Everyone starts calling her Masha in honor of the gloomy women in both *The Seagull* and
Three Sisters—and on account of her Slavic pallor. Behind me a hammy
lesbian lolls in a baroquely outfitted camping chair: "My girlfriend last
night was all, '*SEVEN a.m.?* It's not a rock concert!' And I'm all, 'No, you
don't see, baby. It's the *ultimate* rock concert. Pretend if Mick Jagger
hasn't toured for twenty years, and now he's doing it *gratis.*'"

A middle-aged redhead weaves through the crowd, calling out,
"Anyone wanna make ten bucks?" She's a nurse and she can't get off
work until noon. Would someone be so kind as to hold her place?
Everyone else ignores her, but, temporarily overtaken by heat stroke, I
assent. Masha squints at me, disapproving. By the time the nurse
returns three hours later, I've been through the throes of a major moral
dilemma. I've rehearsed a brief speech, which I sputter nervously: "I
was wrong to agree to this, ma'am. These people have been waiting
here all day, and I'd be cheating them. Not only that, I'd be cheating
myself." I give the word "myself" a breathless little diminuendo, for
gravitas, and point to my sternum, for even more gravitas.

"Relax, honey," she says, unmoved. "Sit back. It's hot. I made some
Tang." She presents a fishbowl containing placenta-like liquid and sits
down next to me. Ripples of malcontent travel down the line. The nurse
tries to redeem herself by offering everyone the drink, which she's
pouring from the fishbowl into little Dixie cups swiped from some
waiting room. Just like that, she has earned the title of Tang Lady. As in,
"Tang Lady thinks she can just waltz in here in front of all these honest
people" and "Tang Lady probably killed that poor goldfish for the
bowl." Even mild-mannered Masha whispers to me: "It only took Tang
Lady ten bucks to buy your soul?" I can't take this. I save my everlast-
ing soul, declining Tang Lady's two sweaty five-dollar bills.

The Pratt folks keep moving our line off the grass, apparently concerned that a Chekhov-crazed mob will tear up the landscaping. During each move several people squeeze ahead in line. An enterprising woman in a golf visor starts dispensing numbers, scrawled on wispy pieces of artist vellum, to mark our place in line. She has nothing to do with the Public Theater or Pratt. She is simply Number 46, a concerned citizen. Whenever someone new arrives, she gives them a number and explains gently that their chances are slim. Everyone looks upon Number 46 with admiration. She is Order; she is Efficiency; she is Florence Nightingale swooping among the invalids.

12:30 p.m., The Pratt Institute

The line has degenerated into a sort of miasmic be-in. Almost everyone here is an artist of some sort. Who else could spend an entire weekday waiting in line? Relaxed in our spots now, no longer defending our territory, we pass the final hour with movie talk. A slender black girl announces, unashamed, that she had the greatest time at *Planet of the Apes*. Ditto *Jurassic Park III*, someone says. Murmurs of assent. Masha, finally living up to her namesake, speaks out: "That is so—God!—typical. A bunch of artists sitting around talking about what summer movies they've been to. If we can't talk about culture, who can?" Everyone looks down at their feet. The lawn sprinklers go *shirr shirr shirr,* making the silence feel longer.

The sun is high, and I've forgotten to bring SPF 50 for my Elizabethan cheeks. I've fashioned a sort of T.E. Lawrence desert headdress out of my shirt. The collar is flipped up, cunningly, to serve as a visor. "We're talking about movies," I offer, "because our culture privileges that medium." This may be the first time I've used "privileges" as a verb, as opposed to "Finish your vegetables or you'll lose your television privileges." I look around. No one seems to have noted a lack of fluency, so I continue: "We can't discuss, say, industrial design or twelve-tone composition in the same way because it doesn't have a universal audience." A man with well-manicured dreadlocks interrupts: "Dude. You're wearing a *shirt* on your *head.*" I do not finish explicating cultural hierarchies in contemporary America. I take the shirt off my head. By the day's end, my face will have turned the color of a bruised beet. Embarrassment Red.

Still trying to redeem our Hollywood coffee klatch, one woman is compelled to describe her own work: "I use nonletter characters— barely pixels, really—in repetition to form expressive landscapes." A man with a sort of butch Peter Lorre accent says that that reminds him of an episode of *Ripley's Believe It or Not!* in which a savant monkey uses a typewriter. The artist, her lips pursed, does not seem delighted by the comparison.

Just then a trio of old ladies bursts into our hipster assembly like Victorian adventuresses among the Ubangi. One of them holds a parasol, canary yellow. Number 46 approaches to tell them the deal. The parasol lady says she heard that "golden girls" get to go to the front of the line. Masha mutters, "That's the problem with New York: All these people with an overdeveloped sense of entitlement, thrown together."

A few feet away a shirtless man in Tevas has started to spread discord. "This isn't going to work," he grumbles. "Everyone's gonna rush to the front, number or no." He even suggests that indefatigable Number 46 has an ulterior motive. "She's probably, like, making herself Number 1 soon as the tickets get here." Teva Guy whips out a black magic marker. He is doctoring his number 75 into a 15, like a schoolboy coaxing a D into a B. "We've got to stop that guy!" says the lesbian in the complicated chair, her eyes flashing. It's turning into that shipwreck movie where everyone kills and eats Shelley Winters. Or am I confusing it with that Chilean soccer team? It's too hot.

1:15 p.m., Still at Pratt

When the Public Theater courier finally arrives with the tickets, there are a good five minutes of teeming and roiling and gnashing of teeth. A woman dumps out her purse, searching for her lost number. An anonymous elbow lands in my ribs. It's hard to tell what's happening. Then, through the melee, a voice, a sweetly authoritarian voice: "Number 11? There you are. Number 12? Great. We're gonna beat this, folks." It is Number 46, calling out our numbers. "Number 13? Do we have an unlucky 13?" She parts the crowd with one hand, shielding the sun from her eyes with the other. We suddenly remember the human inclination toward order. We're the boy savages in *Lord of the Flies*, dropping our spears as the navy ship crests the horizon.

All of a sudden, it's over. A cheerful number 42 and 43 leave arm in arm, waving the last two pink vouchers. That's all, folks.

The masses cry out:

"Forty-three tickets for Brooklyn?"

"That sucks!"

"This is a joke, right?"

"Maybe there'll be a miracle."

No one is leaving. It's been so long since we lived in a world outside of the line. What's it like out there now? Everyone we knew is probably dead. What were we waiting for, anyway? There's no longer anything at the front of the line, yet no one is leaving. Is it possible I've finally become a *regular* somewhere, on a patch of grass in Brooklyn? Could it be that this city is as good at community as it is at anonymity?

There is talk of an après-line party. "And no one with a ticket will be invited!" says a woman who was probably excluded from tree forts as a child. But slowly people start to disperse. Masha and I pass the woman who made it all possible. Number 46. She seems to be in shock. "I was only three people away," she explains, fighting back tears. A small crowd has gathered around her in silent reverence. I start to feel a little misty-eyed.

Masha looks at me and squeezes my hand. "Man, this was the play right here," she says.

THE BREAKFAST CLUB

by Joel Stein

New York stunts your growth. As a kid I assumed that by my late twenties, I'd be an adult, with a wife, kids, a house, patterned china and furniture with red silk tassels hanging from the corners. I was kind of fey as a kid. Still, manhood eludes me like it did Carol Channing. I've tried my best to act like an adult: I've worried about my future; I've thought about my relationships; I even bought a David Sanborn album.

Several months ago, though, a unique opportunity presented itself. The publicist for the Rainbow Room, whom I have trouble talking to because I once told her she had "soft cheeks" (I tend to panic during that cheek-kissing thing), told me of a way to simultaneously exploit and quash my youth: a junior membership at the Club at Rockefeller Center. The place is so desperate for fresh meat that for only $250 a year, they'd let me have a free breakfast in the Rainbow Room at the top of 30 Rock on any weekday I felt like stopping by. The only requirements were that I wear a jacket and be under 35.

I joined with my friend Adam, not just because he's a great guy, but also because he owns a jacket. As it turns out, Adam and I are the only members who are closer to birth than to death. We are also the only ones who ever look out at the view. The others all look bored out of their minds, probably due to those pink British newspapers they're reading. We, on the other hand, take our usual table, gaze out the window at 1,000 feet and squeal, "We're higher than the birds! We're higher than the birds!"

Furthermore, we're the only ones who aren't making business deals while we dine—there's actually a little pad and pen on your table for doing business math. Adam and I just use it to try to calculate how cheap the breakfasts actually are. We figured out that if we came twice a week, divided by 52 weeks, at $250 a year, it would be . . . well, that's where the business math would have come in handy.

I'm further reminded of my failure at passing as an adult when the hosts and coat-check people—our only peers in age and salary—insist on greeting us as "Mr. Sachs" and "Mr. Stein." This makes me so uncomfortable that I cannot conduct a conversation with any of them. Usually I just mumble something like "Keep the change, toots," although there is never any money involved. It's gotten so bad, I've thought about responding to "Hello, Mr. Stein" with "Please, call me Joel." But that sounds even more like I really am someone who should be called Mr. Stein. So I considered responding by saying, "Mr. Stein? Are you crazy? I write penis jokes for a living. And not even for TV. I've got the sexual maturity of a 14-year-old boy. Call me Joel." But Adam talked me out of that one. He had also tried to talk me out of the soft-cheeks comment, so I listen to him now.

Whenever I'm greeted as I enter or leave my little adult space, I'm reminded of the mock "Mr. Stein" I used to hear from Mr. Lutter, my eighth-grade vice principal who once gave me a detention. He accused me of "pussy-footing" around, which made me laugh really hard. So, now, every time I hear "Mr. Stein," I think of Mr. Lutter and realize that I don't want to be an adult, that I don't need to be an adult, and that *pussy-footing* is a really funny word. I'm going to live out this Peter Pan existence as long as I can. Because one day in the not-too-distant future—in fact, probably very, very soon—Adam and I are going to be the *only* Rainbow Room members, and we're going to demand that we not have to wear jackets or be addressed as Mister. Except by the cute hostess who recently dyed her hair blond. I kind of like it when she calls me that.

BUDGET LIVING

- Of course there's the standard Ziploc bag washing, and hitting the dollar bin at the liquor store. But my identical twin/roommate and I have really saved a lot by sharing a profile for our online dating service.

- Eat a peanut butter and jelly sandwich, with a glass of water, for lunch every single weekday for several years running (and no lunch on weekends).

- Shower at the gym to save on shampoo.

- I make up aliases on Craigslist when I want to buy something. I propose a ridiculously low amount, say half their asking price, for the item using an alter ego. Then I e-mail as myself, proposing a more reasonable, yet still largely discounted, price. That way, the seller thinks he's getting a better offer from me and is more willing to sell.

- I used to stalk people with full drinks playing pool or darts in crowded bars. I would wait for them to set down their drinks and look away, and then I'd steal the drinks. Sad, I know, but true.

- At Burger King I order a Whopper, then ask for a packet of barbecue sauce. Instantly, I have a specialty burger at the Whopper price.

- Drink on an empty stomach.

- For one period of my life I lived off of those huge bags of soft pretzels from Costco that cost something like four dollars for two dozen. Pretzels with barbecue sauce, pretzels with spaghetti sauce, pretzels with sugar and cinnamon for dessert, I did it all. It saved time, too—just ten to twenty seconds in the oven, and they were ready.

- I ask cab drivers to let me off a few blocks early to save fifty cents or so.

- Last year I packed ten bottles of Charles Shaw (Two-Buck Chuck) wine in my backpack and brought it as a carry-on when I flew back to New York City from Los Angeles.

- I temped at a huge arbitration/mediation firm in San Francisco, where the judge would order these individually wrapped, gourmet sandwiches for the lawyers and clients. One time I clandestinely took like nine of the leftover sandwiches home with me and put them in the fridge. I was living with my girlfriend's grandparents at the time.

- I ate New York City Chinese food almost exclusively for a month. It was usually a pint of vegetable lo mein for $2.80.

- At some grocery stores they now have self check-out, so for produce you have to key in all of your items. Organic bananas at conventional banana prices!

CO-OP CONFESSIONAL

by Catherine Price

Wednesday, August 28, 7:30 p.m.

I sit on a folding chair in a circle of would-be members, sneaking handfuls of free whole wheat pretzels as I wait my turn to speak. The twenty-three others gathered for orientation are fresh-faced and earnest, dressed in Lands' End and L.L.Bean. When asked their reasons for joining, they mention things like community involvement, raw food diets, and fighting against capitalist systems of consumption.

"I want to join the Park Slope Food Co-op," I say, "because, well, I guess I just want to buy good food at low prices." I glance around nervously—should I mention The Man?—but the orientation leader smiles. I smile back, relieved. I've just graduated from college, where I collected numerous awards for my community-oriented spirit, and have now been thrust into the "real world" where, as far as I can tell, no one really cares if you organize a lot of study breaks. Part of the reason that I'm at the co-op is that I want my community back.

I have my photograph taken for my membership card, without which I won't be allowed to shop. This card is linked to a computerized record of my attendance at mandatory, monthly two-and-three-quarter-hour work shifts. My ID card also shows my member number, which corresponds to a handwritten 4 x 6 index card holding a backup record of my history as a co-op member. I pay my fees, sign up for a work squad, and pick up my complimentary, reusable mesh grocery bag.

And now I am a member—part of a large, loving, organic community—eligible to buy unlimited chemical-free produce at only 20 percent above cost.

Saturday, September 6, 10:34 a.m.
It is my first official visit to the co-op. I swipe my card at the front desk, hand-select my silken tofu, and am ready to pay—a three-step process involving:

a. Waiting in the checkout line (where a worker rings up your groceries, but you can't pay)
b. Waiting in the cashier line (no credit or debit cards, only cash or check)
c. Waiting in the exit line to have both receipts checked and stamped by a "door worker"

Not knowing that there is only one checkout line and that it starts inconspicuously next to the toilet paper, I walk directly up to the next available counter and cut a line so long that it snakes through the frozen food aisle, around the corner, and into bulk spices. My friendly co-op members do not respond kindly to my mistake. "You just cut the entire line," sneers a Dansko clog–wearing mother of twins as she maneuvers her cart in front of mine. "Next time, look behind you."

Thursday, September 26, 8:37 p.m.
It is my first work shift. I have signed up to work as a cashier, taking people's money after the checkout workers have totaled their groceries.

It is an elite position, I am told, since cashiers are the only co-op workers who actually handle cash. Two and a half hours later, I am triple-counting pennies in a windowless basement room. In co-op terms, an "elite" job is one that no one else wants to do.

Thursday, October 31, 7:22 p.m.
It is Halloween. This month I am working at the front door, swiping membership cards. Halfway through my shift, sick of announcing to people that they are on "work alert" for missed shifts, I switch roles with my coworker Elga. Now I am head trick-or-treat coordinator, responsible for giving rewards to a costumed parade of pesticide-free children. Other shops, aware of the urban wives' tale of razor blades being embedded in unwrapped treats, are handing out Tootsie Rolls and mini Snickers bars. We are handing out apples.

A small, androgynous fireman/bear walks up to me and extends its jack-o'-lantern bucket.

"He's adorable," I say to the fireman/bear's mother, just as her child picks an apple out of my bucket and puts it back on the counter.

"I want chocolate," it says.

"We're not giving out chocolate."

"I want chocolate," s/he repeats.

"We only have apples."

"Chocolate!"

"I don't understand," says the mother. "She's been organic since birth."

Thursday, October 31, 9:01 p.m.
I am still at the co-op, three hours after my work shift began, in a meeting led by Harold, my squad leader. Harold ends his e-mails to our

squad with the tagline "Yours in cooperation" and loves holding post-work squad chats in the childcare room, where he has just told us that we will have to reschedule our next two months' work shifts since they fall on Thanksgiving and Christmas, when the co-op will be closed. He then invites us to his annual wassailing party. I suggest that we just skip our work slots, go to his party, and get drunk on eggnog. Elga is the only one who laughs.

Friday, November 29, 3:59 p.m.
This time I try working checkout, scanning shoppers' purchases before they proceed to the cashier. I'm checking people out in both senses of the term, but unfortunately, it turns out that most co-op members are either married, with child, or vegan.

My first customer is a middle-aged woman with short, spiked hair and a T-shirt with a crossed-out image of George W. Bush.

"I know I had a coupon for soy crisps," she says, pulling her wallet out of her bag and rifling through it. "I know it's in here. I brought it in here for the soy crisps."

At first I don't respond; co-op members frequently talk to themselves.

"Where is that coupon? I know I put it in here. It's for soy crisps. Where is it?"

"Are you sure you brought it?" I ask, keying in 94011: organic bananas.

"Oh, I brought it all right. I must have dropped it."

I look at the contents of the woman's cart. There are no soy crisps. I point this out to her, but she isn't dissuaded, still poking through her wallet as the seconds tick by.

"And you know what the worst part of this is?" She glances up at me, eyes gleaming. "I'm missing my yoga class right now. Disco yoga."

"Disco yoga?"

"Oh, yes." She leans in closer to me, conspiratorially. "But you wouldn't understand. You're not a disco duck."

Friday, December 26, 2:38 p.m.

"I'm sorry, honey, I've only got eighty dollars," says the woman at my checkout station, pushing a shopping cart overflowing with Peace Cereal, chicken-free nuggets, and saw palmetto extract "for a healthy prostate." Fortunately, the checkout line, which feeds all eleven checkout desks, starts too far away for people to see what is happening at my station. But still. I have only gotten through her cart's top basket and already she is at sixty-five dollars, with multivitamins and grass-fed meat still to be scanned.

Sure enough, five boxes of soymilk and one free-range chicken later, she is at eighty-two dollars. But rather than admit defeat, she begins to re-evaluate her priorities.

"Do me a favor, honey, and unscan one of those soymilks." I press ITEM VOID on my screen, scroll through the list of products I've already scanned, and deduct one box of Vitasoy from her receipt.

"And take off the chicken. And the bee pollen." Item Void, scroll, delete.

"No, wait, maybe I need the soymilk. Put that one back on. Take off the kale." Done. "Or, wait, maybe the daikon."

Give up! I want to yell. *You have more than two hundred dollars' worth of groceries in that cart! You are only fooling yourself!* But that is not the co-op's way. Seventeen minutes pass as we scan and unscan soymilk, rearrange groceries, discuss her food priorities, talk about her recipe for protein shakes, and ignore the distant checkout line, which has again stretched past biodegradable household cleansers and into frozen foods.

Thursday, January 23, 6:22 p.m.

TO THE MAN WHO BROUGHT FORTY-SEVEN ITEMS TO MY
"EXPRESS" LINE AND THEN WENT ON SEVEN SEPARATE TRIPS
BACK INTO THE STORE FOR ITEMS HE "FORGOT" WHILE I SAT
PASSIVELY AT MY CHECKOUT STATION, KILLING TIME BY READ-
ING THE INGREDIENT LABEL ON HIS ORGANIC OMEGA-3
MAYONNAISE WITH FLAXSEED OIL:

I hate you.

Thursday, February 20, 8:31 p.m.

I have missed my work slot. As a penalty, I have to work two makeups by
my next shift. If I don't, I will have a ten-day grace period before being
suspended from shopping. So will my housemate, Max, who is also
a co-op member. Although we don't share food, our address shows
that we are part of the same household, and he will be found guilty by
association.

I feel so bad about implicating Max that I bump into a woman in
the produce aisle.

"Oh, I'm sorry," I say.

She whirls around. "What are you sorry about?" she says, voice
laced with feminist righteousness. "You have *nothing* to apologize for."

Sunday, February 23, 3:37 p.m.

I am late for my makeup shift and by the time I've signed the attendance log, all of the checkout workers have already been relieved. I am
about to cross my name off the list and come back another time when
an idea hits me: I have already signed in. The store is crowded. I could
walk out without working my shift and *no one would ever know.*

I pat myself on the back for my brilliance and reward my ingenu-
ity by shopping for my own groceries before slipping out the door.

While waiting in the line to pay, I overhear a man say that he is the squad leader, that they don't need any more workers, and that he himself is so busy that he doesn't know when he'll take attendance. *Sweet,* I think to myself. *An alibi.*

Wednesday, February 26, 4:55 p.m.
I am still congratulating myself on my cunning when I stop by the co-op for bananas.

"You're on work alert," the front desk worker tells me.

"Oh, no, I'm not really," I say. "I did my work slot Sunday. They must not have gotten it into the system yet."

The worker looks skeptical, but waves me by.

Friday, February 28, 7:25 p.m.
I am still on work alert.

If this doesn't get cleared up soon, I'm going to have to go to the office.

Monday, March 3, 7:02 p.m.
Shit.

The Food Co-op's office is on the second floor of the building, up a stairway flanked by bulletin boards covered with advertisements (yoga and Pilates, mostly, plus lots of apartment shares with "cat lovers"), past the childcare room and the handicapped-accessible ramp. Lists of work slots cover the walls, and several full-time office workers sit behind iMacs at a long, outward-facing table next to a cabinet holding members' handwritten permanent files.

It doesn't even occur to me to tell the truth.

A woman named Autumn listens to my story and pulls out the attendance log for my supposed makeup shift. Scanning down the names, I recognize my handwriting and point triumphantly to my name, only to notice on second glance that it has a line through it.

"That's weird," I say. "That's my name, but it's crossed out."

"Are you sure you worked the whole shift?" asks Autumn, looking up at me. It is my last chance at honesty.

"Yup. I'm sure I did," I say. "I worked checkout."

"Huh, that's funny." Autumn is now looking at a hand-scribbled note below my name. "It says they tried to find you to take attendance, but couldn't."

My heart begins to beat faster.

"And then this says . . . this says, 'Tried to page member on intercom but had no response. Can only assume that member did not work shift.'" She looks up at me again.

"That's so funny," I repeat, as if the whole concept of the Food Co-op were one big, hysterical joke. "I guess it's just that when I'm working checkout, I, you know, totally space out!" I wave my hands in the air in front of my face to indicate "spaceiness." But Autumn doesn't see me because she is looking back down at the note.

"It says here that they paged you *six* times," she says. "You're saying that you didn't hear *any* of them?"

Six times? The intercom speakers are directly above the checkout area! Granted, most of the pages are from perky-voiced people looking for Asiago cheese and/or trying to hitch rides to Cobble Hill, but still. I decide to call in my alibi. "I talked to the squad leader, though. He said it was a really crazy day!"

"Oh, you talked to the squad leader?" Autumn says, her face radiating hope. "I can just give him a call and ask if he remembers you."

I try to protest, but Autumn is already on the phone, leaving a message for a man I have never actually met. What's more, she has called in Maureen, a permanent staff member who has been hardened by full-time work with evasive members. I have seen Maureen in action and have no doubt that she is personally responsible for the scathing front-page article in the last week's co-op newsletter, the *Linewaiters' Gazette*, about a member who got kicked out for lying to the administrative board. She terrifies me.

Autumn shows Maureen the handwritten note, tells her my story, and both look up at me with critical, quizzical expressions. I smile meekly.

"It can be hard to hear the speakers over the noise at checkout," Maureen says in an unexpected act of kindness, her eyes piercing my guilty, guilty soul. "Just don't let it happen again."

Saturday, March 8, 11:11 a.m.

The co-op is eight blocks from my home. Steve's C-Town grocery, on the other hand, is five and sits directly across the street from my gym. Can I help it if I sometimes step inside?

What worries me is not the act itself, but how good it makes me feel. I walk slowly down the produce aisle, admiring the apples' glossy, waxed skin, shimmering in the store's fluorescent lights, the same lights that radiate upon Boar's Head cold cuts, Jell-O Pudding Snacks, and junk food made with genetically modified corn. There aren't any membership cards to swipe—C-Town is no gated community—and my fellow shoppers' carts burst with mini donuts, ribeye steaks, and nonorganic sausage. When it is time to leave, I browse through the sex tips in *Cosmopolitan* and impulse buy Dentyne Ice from a disaffected clerk, after standing in a single line to both check out *and* pay. The air smells of raw chicken. Ambrosia.

ANOTHER ONE RIDES THE COMETBUS

by Jessica Nordell

I was thirteen when I saw the blurb in the back of a magazine, just a few lines wedged alongside a black-and-white photo of a Xeroxed and slightly pained-looking face. I had just crossed to the winning side of a sweet babysitting deal that had netted me six dollars in exchange for two hours spent eating refrigerated Twinkies while babykins slept upstairs. So I tucked a wrinkled dollar bill into an envelope and sent away for what the tiny blurb described as a "zine," from California, put out by some guy named Aaron Cometbus.

I'd all but forgotten about it when, two weeks later, a slim manila envelope showed up in the mailbox, stuffed between *Kiplinger's Personal Finance* and "You May Have Already Won a Million Dollars!" My name and address were printed in messy, block letter Sharpie, and inside the envelope were one hundred and ten handwritten, photocopied pages, stapled together into a miniature magazine about the size of a package of presliced ham. This was *Cometbus*: it was tiny and homemade, and it clanged into my life like an emergency, all sirens blaring.

Let me back up. I had just started eighth grade in a midsize town in northeastern Wisconsin. Our house was halfway between a cemetery and a prison, and aside from the occasional sit-in my friends and

I organized in the middle school cafeteria, life was pretty uneventful. We'd pass notes in science class—updating, Wikipedia-style, the story of Jason and Sarah's attempt to have sex in the woods near Green Isle Park. (According to our sources, it "didn't work.") On weekends we'd slink around Godfather's Pizza in the mostly abandoned strip mall near my house, trying out crude stand-up routines on the surly clerks behind the counter. The late summer days rolled forward like the wheels of a combine. In the muggy afternoons we'd toss pennies into the dried-up fountain at the mall, or lie on the living room carpet with our eyes closed, listening to the low bellow of the paper mill across the river.

But then, every once in a while, apropos of almost nothing, a feeling would bloom in my chest. I'd be sitting on my bed, listening to a rock song, and a flame would swirl up and go skittering along the length of my bones: There was something else out there. I *felt* it. Something sparkly, concentrated, dazzling. Things were supposed to glow. Things were supposed to—I don't know—*happen*. It had only been a couple of years since I'd shown up at school wearing a green sweat suit with dinosaurs emblazoned on it in puffy paint (a major strategic error, but that's another story), and already childhood was fading out of view. I was halfway down the muddy footpath between being a kid and . . . something else. What? Glory? Beauty? Heat death, said the days. Orthodontia, said my mother.

But now, there it was, exploding out from the pages of *Cometbus* #24: that *something else*. It was something I'd glimpsed maybe once or twice before. I'd seen it when I visited my musician cousin in pre-Giuliani New York, his girlfriend's skeleton collection taking up an entire room of their apartment. I'd sniffed it at the punk shows I snuck out to see at the condemned theater downtown, where shadowy twenty-year-olds draped themselves on the rotting velvet staircase. And it sounds sort of crazy to say that the heavy wooden door between my daily existence and the largeness of life itself was thrust open forever by a photocopied magazine. But there it is.

Adulthood, *Cometbus*-style, had normal adult stuff in it—jobs, responsibilities, relationships—but, the magazine seemed to exclaim, *That's incidental to the mad glee of being around to experience any of it at all.* Adulthood was bizarre and silly and unhinged, and lots could be accomplished, with style, for next to nothing. That issue was filled with rambling prose pieces about bathrooms in L.A., reviews of cereal brands, and aggressive surrealism—weird S&M photos pasted next to an interview with a guy named Mickey Creep, fashion models photocopied to inscrutability and given speech bubbles full of hieroglyphics. There were cooking tips, sewing tips, scary comic strips, slang glossaries, and a profile of "that bearded guy at Rasputin's."

And then there were how-to guides, like "25 Fun Things to Do for Free," which included hanging around junkyards and enjoying the "postapocalyptic beyond-Thunderdome atmosphere," auditing random classes at Berkeley, and the somewhat less likely (but according to the penciled star next to it, my thirteen-year-old self's favorite), "Pretend everyone is a bloodsucking freak chasing after you and run from them screaming." There was an advice column called "Ask Kent"—with a photo of a cheerful nine-year-old (Kent, presumably)—and questions like, "Where do biology teachers get those weird things in jars?" "Where is the heartland?" and "Are any of the famous musicians behind bars in jail bands?"

A story called "The Night I Almost Met Darby Crash" (the Germs front man who started doing music when he was kicked out of college for "antisocial behavior") began, "Me and my sort-of ex-girlfriend Linda were having this contest to see who was more punk, and she thought she had it all wrapped up when she started hanging out with

Nancy the Jewish lesbian skinhead." There was an interview with Mark Hosler, of the eighties experimental rock band Negativland, in which he mentions (attention rock historians!) some new outtakes he has of "Casey Kasem saying really nasty things about U2" and describes his plan to make a "really horrendous home stereo version of 'I Still Haven't Found What I'm Looking For.'"

This was a magazine put out by adults, real live people supporting themselves, paying rent, driving around—probably, I imagined, in '69 Chevy Malibus—adults for whom the unruly world was something to adore, something to fall in love with over and over again. *Cometbus* knew that anyone, anywhere, could have a story, a lesson, a warning— it loved hobos and dreamers, autodidacts and trespassers. Granted, the "adults" who wrote for and were written about in *Cometbus* were probably nineteen. Maybe twenty-two. But to me they seemed like wise angels, otherworldly creatures who had something to teach me about how to navigate the dense, stuffy world.

The themes and capers that surfaced again and again—hanging around Dumpsters, talking with strangers about their bands/road trips/conspiracy theories, having people tell you things you're not sure are true, having people tell you things you're *sure* are not true— had something in common. Call it a Dumpster ethos, salvaging trash and finding it beautiful. *Cometbus*—its writers, its readers—loved the ugly, the weird, and even the things that never happen at all (the writer, after all, never did meet Darby Crash). In *Cometbus*land, every story, no matter how bizarre, depressing, or outrageous, was told with pride and finesse because even when bad things happen—and if you live with any sense of adventure, bad things are bound to happen— you can use them to tell one hell of a story.

There's a tiny coda at the end of issue #24 called "Every Town Is a Lousy Town." It's an anonymous account of one woman's exquisitely

bad month abroad—from customs on, she says, "clouds of ill conse-
quence were firmly fixed to my body." Within days, she was frostbitten
and broke; the highlight of Austria, she writes with gallows humor, was
"attempting suicide in my cold hotel room." By the end of the trip, she
says, she's lost her health, her mind, and her money, and when she
finally returns home in a state of exhaustion and shock, she finds that
many people didn't even know she'd been gone.

And it's true—many people don't know we're gone, or here, or
anywhere, and there's nothing we can do except tell our stories when
we get back. After my *Cometbus* epiphany, eighth grade continued,
Efren punched out the cafeteria window, I toted around a raggedy
leather bowling bag—but I wasn't the person I'd been, and I'd probably never be her again. My insides had exploded; the inkling I'd had
about possibilities had bloomed into a Rorschach splotch coating my
whole worldview. I had something to look forward to, and even better, I
had partners out there in the universe, even if we didn't know each
other yet, even if we never would. *Cometbus* opened a world to me that
I'd only peeked at through the slats of someone else's fence. It showed
me that what was waiting on the other side of childhood was a cabinet
of curiosity and delight—found love letters, seedy musicians, toothless sages, curried rice—and it helped me put one foot inside.

Now, fifteen years later, I'm unquestionably an adult, and I've hit
my head on the real world a few times. During college it was easy to live
out *Cometbus*'s vagabond bohemian dream: I befriended a guy who
lived in a closet in the hallway of my freshman dorm. I ate cast-off
mangoes from the downtown Boston farmers' market. I stayed out all
night scouring the neighborhood for discarded furniture and listened
with rapt attention when a friend described how he had scaled the
two-hundred-foot-tall CITGO sign that rises up over the Charles River.

But then, sometime in my early twenties, my daily life began to teeter uncomfortably close to the fringe, and security and routine seemed less like conventions to be resisted than comforts rapidly receding from my grasp. After college I moved home for a while and, for the first time in my life, felt completely at sea. My friends went off to get master's degrees in Central European history; I got a job at the perfume counter of a local department store. On my breaks I'd go into the supply room and find props to create dioramas for the perfume displays. For Escape perfume I created a desert jail scene, using bronzing powder from the makeup counter for sand. For Contradiction, I put together a miniature bondage scene, wrapping the perfume in dampened tissue paper, twisted into gauzy strips. I thought they looked great. I was asked to leave a few days later.

I found another job as an "agent" for a local watercolorist who wanted to increase the sales of her lithographs. She employed me to drive around town and persuade galleries to carry her work—and also to accompany her to the country club for fruit compote and club sandwiches. Most of the galleries specialized in paintings of Green Bay Packers in various triumphant poses; when I set a lithograph of St. Mark's Church on the counter, they looked at me like I had lost my mind. Maybe I had. I pictured myself living in the closet of a freshman dorm for the rest of my life, surviving on soggy egg salad sandwiches and bowls of gelatinous fruit. I watched my peers move into stable jobs and stable lives, and the mainstream started to look pretty good.

But even as I bounced from misstep to mistake, I carted (a now-pretty-shabby-looking) *Cometbus* around with me and kept its ideals in the back of my mind—ideals that, over time, had less to do with off-the-grid-bohemianism and more to do, simply, with an underlying spirit of self-determination. (During a buttoned-down job interview downtown it dawned on me that wearing a yellow acrylic sweater with appliquéd daisies and the words APRIL SHOWERS BRING MAY FLOWERS embroidered on the sleeve might not be the most effective way to demonstrate my creativity.)

A few months ago I gave up the security of a full-time job to free-lance as a writer. While my family carefully reviewed the various short-comings of this plan, the tattered magazine still sitting on my bookshelf gave me, at least in part, the courage to actually do it. And in a way, being a writer is more in the spirit of the magazine than adopt-ing a lipstick found in the back of a taxicab ever was: My job is to go into the world, to listen and watch, and to assess everything I see on its own terms.

When I was thirteen I thought what *Cometbus* did was show me that the world *held* something specific, and that all I had to do was search out those particular treasures, hidden in its folds. But I think what it really did was offer a point of view—about possibility and won-der, and even about love. The world, after all, is always the same: It holds as much magic or drudgery as we see from our vantage point. And maybe adulthood is simply that—that realization. From start to finish, it cost me a dollar—not quite like finding it in a Dumpster, but awfully close.

LAST TWENTY-FOUR HOURS IN NEW YORK

by Rachel Hutton and Christina Amini

After college we moved to New York and got nine-to-five jobs, and after two years we decided the working world wasn't, well . . . working. Christina had recently come across an old list of "Things I Want to Be When I Grow Up." Online marketing manager was not on the list. Neither was project coordinator. So we did what we had to do: We quit our jobs without getting new ones first.

Unable to afford living in New York City unemployed—and desperate to find out if what we'd do for money could overlap with what we'd do for love—we sublet the apartment and decided to move back to our parents' houses, just for the summer (or so we thought). Leaving meant leaving behind all that makes New York an irreplaceable home: its struggles, its surprises, and its sidewalks littered with chicken bones.

June 3, 2001

RACHEL	**CHRISTINA**

8:03 a.m.

Wake up to a light gray haze. Minor spurts of anxiety. Make mental to-do list. Lie on bare mattress inside sleeping bag for a few more minutes to collect thoughts.

8:32 a.m.

Wake up in my girlfriend's tiny bedroom. Ellie's still sleeping, her childhood blankie tucked beneath her head.

9:18 a.m.

Call friends who will not be awake to answer the phone. Leave a message telling them I won't be able to go out with them tonight. I have already given them hugs and said my good-byes and I can't handle the awkwardness of saying the same good-byes again.

9:22 a.m.

Call Rachel. Tell her I will be home from Ellie's in five minutes to help clean the apartment.

RACHEL	CHRISTINA
10:09 a.m.	
Wash walls in kitchen for the first time since moving in. Sweep and mop living room and bedroom floors for good subletter karma. Clean windows and dust windowsills with an old sock. This is also the first time. It shows.	
	10:22 a.m.
	Still at Ellie's apartment. Cry. Notice the picture of us at Coney Island tacked up on the fridge alongside a six-month anniversary card. What will happen when we're long distance? Cry again.
11:02 a.m.	
Dust off TV.	
	11:22 a.m.
	Gather remaining stuff from Ellie's apartment: Mirah CD case, one orange sock, hair clips, yesterday's clothes.
11:54 a.m.	
Putter.	
	12:04 p.m.
	Arrive at apartment. Tear off the AMINI/HUTTON label from underneath doorbell.

RACHEL	CHRISTINA

12:09 p.m.

Stomp on one last roach as it scuttles out from under kitchen sink.

12:18 p.m.

Leave self-addressed, stamped envelope with request for subletters to send mail.

12:37 p.m.

Lunch. Enjoy the challenge of creating a meal constrained by the eclectic contents of our refrigerator: blue cheese, half a can of chickpeas, tomato juice.

12:41 p.m.

Eat lunch off of paper towel to avoid washing dishes.

1:20 p.m.

Make our third trip to Goodwill this week. We meet Ellie on the way there. When most couples greet each other, it's often with "How was your day?" When we meet Ellie at her apartment, three blocks away, Christina asks, "How was your hour?"

RACHEL	CHRISTINA
	1:36 p.m.
	Rachel forces me to donate my library card catalog drawers. She says I need to purge. She doesn't know I've already shipped three garage-sale typewriters back to California.
1:55 p.m.	
Arrive at Goodwill drop-off center. Greeted by mangy mutt who drools on our donations. Piles of clothes are scooped into a machine that compresses them into clothing "bales." Bales are swathed to pallets and moved by forklifts.	
	3:14 p.m.
	Take Ellie's bike to a repair shop. (What else would you do on your last day in New York?) Ellie is grumpy, reticent. She walks a few paces ahead of us. She shoves the bike over the subway turnstile with nothing but brute force.
4:17 p.m.	
Head to Canal Street to purchase "I (Heart) NY" baby Ts. Haggle with vendor.	
	5:11 p.m.
	Krispy Kreme. A deal if you buy six. We eat two hot donuts each.

RACHEL

7:07 p.m.

It's raining hard. Raincoat and umbrella already on a UPS truck somewhere in the Midwest. Remove shower curtain with cute goldfish print. Wear it as a rain cape.

8:19 p.m.

Arrive at my friend Lauren's apartment for a birthday celebration. We snack on those delicious little spinach triangles.

9:40 p.m.

Bail out of conversations before getting the "So, what do you do?" question.

CHRISTINA

7:14 p.m.

Meet old friend for tea at a place in the West Village with a fireplace. Remove wet shoes to expose unmatched pair of socks. Dry feet by fire.

9:32 p.m.

My friend asks me about my plans for California. I've taken the GRE, applied to two grad programs, and am considering consulting (in what, I don't know). He convinces me to apply for teaching jobs in New York next year.

RACHEL	CHRISTINA
	9:54 p.m.
	My teacher-friend recounts series of lawyer-mediated parent conferences. Decide not to become a teacher after all.
5:08 a.m.	
Wake up to static on radio alarm clock. Thick fog. No view of the city. Church steeple on neighboring block completely invisible.	
	5:15 a.m.
	I say good-bye to the apartment by patting each surface. Good-bye, room I painted the color of a grapefruit. Bye, cockroach-free cabinet that I sealed up with caulk.
5:26 a.m.	
Stuff alarm clock in suitcase. Sit on suitcase to close latches.	
	5:37 a.m.
	Car service to the airport. Rachel, her three bags, my four bags, Ellie, and I load into the minivan. The air is still foggy. Our driver goes alarmingly fast.

RACHEL	CHRISTINA

RACHEL

5:44 a.m.

Christina shares remarks an author once made about writing: "It's like driving with the headlights on. You can only see ten feet ahead, but that's all you need."

CHRISTINA

6:48 a.m.

Ellie and I give Rachel a hug and kiss good-bye.

7:14 a.m.

Heft my forty-pound sewing machine "carry-on" through the airport despite disparaging looks from baggage screeners. It barely fits through X-ray machine. Open sewing machine for inspector. Thread, bobbins, and scissors scatter on the airport carpet.

7:15 a.m.

It's hard to let go of Ellie. The security guard honks and shouts, "Hurry it up, ladies." We make an agreement: This is just the beginning of the next chapter.

7:55 a.m.

Take off through the clouds. Not much of a view of the city. Can't see where I'm going, and can't see what I'm missing yet.

THINGS TO DO BEFORE THE MORTGAGE

- Enjoy the Zen state brought on by a single-digit bank account balance.

- Renounce your college vegetarianism.

- Live somewhere where drinking in public parks isn't just legal, but is a primary form of social life.

- Travel: When you get older, it is generally *not okay* to sleep out in a city park, chase a Spanish bull with a rolled-up newspaper, go home with drunk foreigners wearing wigs, eat lamb's brain in a Bedouin tent, pay a small child to clean your ears in public, get kidnapped in Morocco, get scabies in Ireland, etc.

- Get into some form of cult entertainment (e.g., *Evil Dead*, Tolkien, "Battlestar Galactica").

- Get renter's insurance.

- Develop a plan to consistently give to charity, rather than the consistent donation to the unused gym membership.

- Don't go to grad school.

- Wake up in places where you have no idea how you got there, with people you don't know (e.g., on the number 49 bus, traveling down Mission Street).

- Buy the one thing that anyone with any sense would never let you buy, so you'll already have it should you meet that person.

- At least once, get rid of most of what you own, and be surprised how easy it is.

- Live in New York City for at least a year.

- Date someone for a long time (to see what you do and don't want in a relationship), and when you break up with him or her, be slutty for a short time.

- Visit all fifty states.

- Freak out, quit your job, and move to Montana. Wait, no, I don't really recommend that.

- Live out of your car.

- Call it like you see it.

- Work on being at peace with the fact that there may never be a mortgage.

CONTRIBUTORS

Thomas Beller is the author of *How to Be a Man, The Sleep-Over Artist,* and *Seduction Theory.* A lifelong resident of New York City, he is a cofounder and editor of *Open City* magazine and creator of the Web site www.mrbellersneighborhood.com.

Shoshana Berger is the founder and editor in chief of *ReadyMade* magazine. Her first book, *ReadyMade: How to Make [Almost] Everything,* was published by Random House. She married the It Guy on April Fools' Day 2006.

Since graduating from college in 1998, **Carson Brown** has lived in six apartments in northern California and Mexico and worked more than thirty different jobs. Soon she hopes to enter medical school to become an integrative physician when she grows up. In the meantime, she is learning to brew beer, identify edible plants, and meditate for more than one minute. She cohabitates happily with her family in Novato, California.

Sasha Cagen is the author of *Quirkyalone: A Manifesto for Uncompromising Romantics* (HarperSanFrancisco) and founder of International Quirkyalone Day, a growing alternative to Valentine's Day that celebrates all forms of love on February 14. She is also the founding editor of *To-Do List*, a magazine of meaningful minutiae, and is currently at work on a book of to-do lists. For more information on her projects, visit www.quirkyalone.net and www.todolistblog.com.

Anna Chlumsky is an actress living in New York City. After an early career in show biz, she received a bachelor degree from the University of Chicago and studied at the Atlantic Theater Company in Chelsea. When not acting, Anna writes screenplays and immerses herself in comic books.

Meghan Daum is the author of the novel *The Quality of Life Report* and the essay collection *My Misspent Youth*. She has contributed to National Public Radio's *Morning Edition* and *This American Life* and has written for numerous publications, including the *New Yorker*, *Harper's*, *GQ*, *Vogue*, *Self*, *New York*, *Radar*, *BlackBook*, *Harper's Bazaar*, the *Village Voice*, the *New York Times Book Review*, and the *Los Angeles Times*. She currently lives in Los Angeles.

Opal Desaire lives in Denver and works in cash management. She is leery of taking vacations with new people and is still in search of Prince Charming.

A product of the Washington, D.C. suburbs, **Sarah Eisenstein** has been living in Brooklyn for six years. In addition to working as a freelance writer, she coordinates the adult literacy program at Brooklyn's IMANI HOUSE and is hoping to be an active member of her tenants' association someday.

Tim Gihring lives in Minneapolis and works as a writer for *Minnesota Monthly* magazine. His work has appeared in *Utne*, the *Japan Times*, and the *San Francisco Chronicle*. He is neither fake nor dating.

Brian Grivna spent two years teaching English in the public schools of Sapporo, Japan. While there, he developed a severe pachinko addiction that ultimately left him penniless. He currently resides in Minneapolis, rebuilding his bankroll as a software engineer.

Jordan Harrison's plays include *Finn in the Underworld* (Berkeley Repertory Theatre), *Kid-Simple* (Humana Festival), and *The Museum Play*. A resident playwright at New Dramatists, Jordan has received fellowships from the Jerome Foundation, the McKnight Foundation, and the NEA/TCG Playwright-in-Residence Program. He grew up in Seattle, lives in Minneapolis, and heard *The Seagull* wasn't that great anyway.

Pagan Kennedy has authored seven books, and has two more forthcoming. She has written for the *New York Times Magazine*, the *Boston Globe Magazine*, *Dwell*, *Utne*, and many other publications. Her most recent nonfiction book was named a *New York Times* Notable of 2002 and a Massachusetts Book Award winner.

Not long after walking off the pipe-counting "legal" job, **David Kolek** enrolled in law school where, much to his disappointment, there have been no pipe-counting classes. He has also written three novels, none of which have been published, despite putting his best face forward. He lives in San Francisco.

Ariana Lamorte is a writer, mother, and teacher whose work has appeared in the *San Francisco Chronicle Magazine*. Her most recent play, *Transition, Transition*, chronicles the unsettled lives of twenty-somethings and has been performed at the Neighborhood Playhouse in New York City and City Lights Theater in San Jose, California. She lives with her husband and son in San Anselmo, California.

Thisbe Nissen is the author of two novels, *Osprey Island* and *The Good People of New York*, and a story collection, *Out of the Girls' Room and into the Night*. She is also the coauthor (with Erin Ergenbright) of *The Ex-Boyfriend Cookbook*. A native New Yorker and a graduate of Oberlin College and the Iowa Writers' Workshop, Thisbe now lives, writes, teaches, gardens, and collages in Iowa City, Iowa.

Jessica Nordell is a writer who lives in Minneapolis. She has worked as a sketch comedy writer for *A Prairie Home Companion* and produced the *Literary Friendships* public radio series for Minnesota Public Radio.

Catherine Price is an essayist, freelance writer, and founder/editor of *Salt* magazine (www.saltmag.net). When not stressing out about the effect that higher interest rates will have on her ability to ever own a home, she's working on a book of personal essays about her attempts to become a real grown-up.

Evan Ratliff's reporting and humor writing have appeared in the *New Yorker, Wired, ReadyMade,* and other shiny publications. He rents in San Francisco.

Davy Rothbart is the creator of *FOUND* magazine, a regular contributor to public radio's *This American Life*, and author of the story collection *The Lone Surfer of Montana, Kansas*. His work has been featured in the *New York Times* and *High Times*. He lives in Ann Arbor, Michigan.

Barbara Rushkoff is a writer and stay-at-home mom. Yes, you can be both. She lives in Brooklyn, New York, with her husband, Douglas, and daughter, Mamie.

Joel Stein is a Sunday op-ed columnist for the *Los Angeles Times* and a contributing writer at *Time*. He also writes for the ABC sitcom *Crumbs*. He grew up in Edison, New Jersey, attended Stanford University, and is both a landlord (N.Y.C.) and a renter (L.A.). Joel claims he has the smallest mortgage of anyone he knows.

Sarah Vowell is the author of *Assassination Vacation, The Partly Cloudy Patriot, Take the Cannoli,* and *Radio On*. She is a contributing editor for public radio's *This American Life*. She is also a McSweeney's person and the voice of teenage superhero Violet Parr in Pixar Animation Studios' *The Incredibles*. She lives in New York City.

Ethan Watters is the author of three books, most recently *Urban Tribes,* which is being developed into a feature film by Warner Bros. His nonfiction has been published widely in such publications as the *New York Times Magazine, Wired,* and *GQ*.

ACKNOWLEDGMENTS

Special thanks to our editor, Beth Bracken, and the rest of the team at Simon Spotlight Entertainment; our agents/angels, Nina Collins and Matthew Elblonk; and our rock star essayists and list-makers. Thanks to those who supported *Before the Mortgage* as a zine: designer Kirk Roberts and all our contributors, subscribers, and cheerleaders.